GIVE IT AWAY

RED HOT CHILI PEPPERS

THE STORIES BEHIND EVERY SONG

ROB FITZPATRICK

CARLTON
BOOKS

This is a Carlton book

First published by in Great Britain by Carlton Books Limited 2004
20 Mortimer Street
London W1T 3JW

Text and Design copyright © Carlton Books Limited 2004

ISBN 1 84442 796 X

Project editor: Lorna Russell
Picture research: Steve Behan
Art Editor: Zoe Dissell
Design: Adam Wright
Cover design: Alison Tutton
Production: Lisa Moore

The publishers would like to thank the following sources for their
kind permission to reproduce the pictures in this book.

Corbis Images: Henry Diltz: 30, 31, 72; /Lynn Goldsmith: 24, 28;
/Fabio Nosotti: 13; /Neal Preston: 8, 50, 60-61, 84; /S.I.N.: 36, 75 , 90

London Features International: Kristin Callahan: 75; /F.Forcino: 74;
/Andrew Galdino: 80; /J. Goedefroit: 41; /Mike Hashimoto: 46; /Joe
Hughes: 42; /Paul Smith: 104

Redferns: Paul Bergen: 41; /Michael Linssen: 78; /Albert Ortega: 67;
/Ebet Roberts: 27, 32; /Jon Super: 73

Retna Pictures Ltd: Sebastian Artz: 119; David Atlas: 128r; /A.J.
Barratt: 39, 55, 57; /Paul Beauchemin: 53; /Bob Berg: 106-7; Jay
Blakesberg: 54, 83; /Kevin P. Casey: 109; /Bernaded Dexter: 63;
/James and James: 69; /Steve Jennings: 103; /Bernhard Kuhmstedt:
14-15; /Robert Matheu: 17, 69, 70; /Clay McBride: 49, 96, 118, 128l;
/Richard Reyes: 22, 108; /Clemens Rikken/Sunshine: 43; RIP: 18;
/Anthony Saint James: 78, 98, 100, 121; Michael Schrieber: 20, 64;
/Debbie Smyth: 130; Robert Spencer:126, 127; /Patricia
Steur/Sunshine: 40; /Andy Teacher: 114; /Neils Van Iperen: 92, 93, 95

Rex Features: 125r, 131; /Dave Allocca: 110-111; /Bjorkman: 116;
/Fotex: 5, 34, 56, 58; /Fotos International: 68; Ixo/Avantis: 85; Lindsay
Maggs: 91; Pasquale Modica: 122; Erik C. Pendzich: 23, 113; /Brian
Rasic: 9, 87, 88, 117, 125l, 132, 135

Wireimage.com: Steve Eichner: 6, 10

Every effort has been made to acknowledge correctly and contact
the source and/or copyright holder of each picture and Carlton
Books Limited apologises for any unintentional errors or
omissions which will be corrected in future editions of this book.

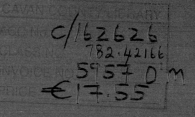

「Contents」

Introduction

Raised in LA's subterranean punk clubs, how did America's strangest group break into the mainstream and become one of the biggest rock bands in the world?

At home in America, they fly the flag for the punk spirit while simultaneously filling arenas and shifting albums by the million – a feat Nirvana's Kurt Cobain tragically found too onerous to maintain. In Japan in 2002, they headlined Fuji Rock and have sold out the Budokan three nights on the trot. Across Europe, they are welcomed almost as one of our own: conquering heroes in the charts and selling out the largest venues. The whole world loves the Red Hot Chili Peppers.

That the Chili Peppers are a multi-platinum-selling, sure-fire, bona-fide rock'n'roll mega-group is obvious. MTV rotates their videos so heavily that viewers probably can't conceive of a time when they couldn't see one of the band's long string of hits at least once an hour and music fans the world over have soaked up their albums in their millions. Tracks like their punk-funk take on Stevie Wonder's classic "Higher Ground", rap-rock genius like, "Give It Away" and international classics like "Under The Bridge" and "The Zephyr Song" only add to their potency.

But it wasn't always this way. The story of the Chili Peppers' 25-year climb from being just another bunch of kids in a school band in Los Angeles goofing around playing Kiss cover versions, to global mega-group, is one of almost constant disaster. At every turn and every apparent breakthrough, the Red Hot Chili Peppers found themselves facing another mountain to climb, dealing with another body blow that might have proved fatal for most other groups.

What has seen them through their troubles, and ultimately rewarded them, is an overwhelming spiritual commitment to the band. It wasn't that they wanted to be big stars and drive around in flash cars, playing the rich rock star role. They were always too punk for that to be their driving force. To be in the Red Hot Chili Peppers is to live the life of the free and the funky. It's about loving Jimi Hendrix and George Clinton equally. It's about being in possession of an almost casual musical virtuosity. It's about mushing together rock, rap, funk and jazz. It's about having a fat black tattoo of the band's chunky star logo on the inside of your arm. It's about California. And it's about paying homage to The Beatles by being photographed walking across Abbey Road with your cock in a sock.

At the heart of this extraordinary story, and at the core of the Chili Peppers' success, is the friendship of two men: Anthony Kiedis (aka Antwon The Swan, aka Anton) and Michael Balzary (aka Flea, aka Mike B the Flea), forged in school and maintained through 25 years of dizzying rock'n'roll excess. This is their story, and the story of their extraordinary Organic Anti-Beatbox Band.

1

The Red Hot Chili Peppers

Anthony Kiedis was born to be a rock star. He arrived on November 1, 1962, in Grand Rapids, Michigan, to parents Margaret and John Kiedis who separated when he was still very young. Anthony lived with his mum until he was 11. It was a fairly typical suburban upbringing, with the exception that whereas most divorced dads worked locally in regular jobs, Anthony's lived in Los Angeles and appeared on TV. Anthony's dad was an actor who went under the exotic alias of Blackie Dammett, and regular phone calls from glamorous LA would inform Anthony, stuck in miserable Michigan, which TV programmes he would be appearing on.

The movie scene of Los Angeles in the early 1970s was a drug-addled round of constant partying. Control of Hollywood had been wrestled away from the studios by maverick talents such as Martin Scorsese, Francis Ford Coppola and Roman Polanski. Hollywood was making edgy, paranoid films, attacking the government over the war in Vietnam and the Watergate scandal, while simultaneously shovelling enough cocaine up its collective nostrils to finance several communist guerilla revolutions in more than one South American republic.

The liberal Hollywood scene took up the sexual revolution of the 1960s with considerable enthusiasm. From the birth of the popular movie in the 1920s, the insular world of the Hollywood film industry had always been where the best parties were, and wild orgies of sex and drugs had been a staple of the average night out for anyone connected to the industry for decades. But in the 1970s, post-hippy, post-Beatles and post-LSD, the lid was off. With the war in Vietnam, where young American men were being slaughtered by the thousand, and the fearsome prospect of nuclear war with the Soviet Union scaring the world witless, the Hollywood cocoon of the 1970s was particularly unhinged.

Anthony's dad, Blackie Dammett, lived the life of the bit-part Hollywood actor to the full. Long-haired and moustached, he appeared in countless TV programmes, including Starsky & Hutch, Charlie's Angels and Magnum P.I., usually as a "heavy". But Blackie was ultimately far more interested in getting laid, taking drugs and partying with his showbiz pals than in acting. Anthony later described his father as a "super freak, an over-the-edge playboy on Sunset Strip". In 1973 his parents made the decision that the boy would move to LA to live with his dad. The moment Anthony left Grand Rapids, Michigan, he left the straight life behind forever.

Blackie saw no reason why having a young boy in his care should curtail his lifestyle any, and his son blended right in to the wild party scene of Blackie's LA life. Anthony started living the uncensored Bacchanalian existence of sex and drugs that would become one of the central platforms of the faith of the Red Hot Chili Peppers. "I lived in a world which contained lots of naked partying girls, lots of drugs, lots of loud music, lots of late night parties, lots of fast cars and lots of Bulgarian albino midgets," he said later.

Also trawling around the party scene of mid-1970s Hollywood was one of Blackie's showbiz pals – Sonny Bono. Bono was a singer/songwriter and a veteran of the LA music scene. He'd started out in the 1950s as an A&R director at Specialty Records and maintained a stop/start writing and recording career of his own in parallel. In 1963 he met Cherilyn La Pierre, since better known as Cher, and the pair embarked on a singing career that delivered one enormous hit – "I Got You Babe" – in 1965. Bono became a great friend for Anthony and provided the steadying influence his own father never could.

"Anthony and I fondly remember long-time friend Sonny Bono," Blackie Dammett later told the Chili

Peppers' fanzine *Rockinfreakapotamus*. "My ex-girlfriend Connie introduced 12-year-old Anthony to Sonny back when Sonny and Cher had the number one rated show on television, and their Las Vegas act sold out concerts around the world. Sonny adored little Tony and took him along on their whirlwind showbiz ride as well as their vacations, which ironically included skiing at Tahoe where Sonny tragically died. We even used Sonny's Bel Air address to get Anthony into a better junior high school and Sonny spent as much time bailing him out of the principal's office as I did."

For a while, it looked like "little Tony" might follow dad on to the silver screen. With Blackie and Sonny encouraging him, and under his stage name of Cole Dammet, Anthony starred as Sly Stallone's son Kevin Kovak in the union-bashing flop, *F.I.S.T.* In 1978 he appeared in *Jokes My Folks Never Told Me*, a teenage sexploitation movie every bit as bad as *Kentucky Fried Movie*. But it would be at school, not on a movie set, where Anthony's life would change forever and the Red Hot Chili Peppers would be born.

In the late 1970s, Hollywood's famous Fairfax High School was a fairly liberal place, but for a boy who had been living Anthony's twilight party life, any high school would represent a considerable change of pace.

"I definitely came into school with a 'fuck the masses' approach," he told *Guitarist* magazine. "While everyone was wearing O.P. gear and listening to Led Zeppelin, it was just too common and popular for me. So I went completely against it. I dressed awkwardly and listened to David Bowie, Benny Goodman, Blondie and all this weird stuff that my dad was turning me onto – just intentionally not to be part of the masses."

It was this desire to be a one-man awkward squad that first attracted Anthony to another Fairfax outsider, Michael "Flea" Balzary. Born in Melbourne, Australia on October 16 1962, Flea also came from a broken home – his parents divorced and his mother

MICHAEL "FLEA" BALZARY first met Kiedis at Fairfax High School, where they were both pupils.

had remarried and moved to America by the time Michael was five. Michael's new stepdad was Walter Urban Jr, a trumpet-playing jazz musician, and the family lived in New York until moving to LA in 1973 when Michael was 11. By this age he was already playing the drums and the trumpet, and in his bohemian jazz home he would jam with his stepdad and his pals.

At school Balzary was small, hence the nickname Flea, and he had a peculiar accent thanks to his Australian background. Flea preferred playing trumpet and listening to Dizzy Gillespie to rock music, which made him something of a weirdo at Fairfax, and among the kids who picked on him was one Jack Irons. And Jack Irons had a mate called Hillel Slovak. Jack (born in California, July 18, 1962) and Hillel (born in Haifa, Israel, April 13, 1962; his family moved to Los Angeles in 1967) were, like several million teenagers growing up in America in the late 1970s, huge fans of the theatrical rock outfit Kiss. They

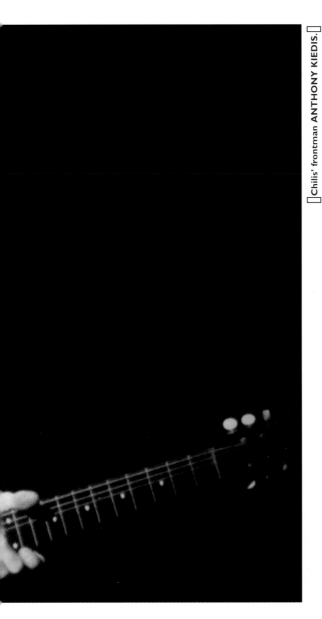

to playing guitar. Together with fellow Fairfax pupils Alain Johannes (already an accomplished guitar player) and Todd Strasman on bass, Hillel and Jack formed Chain Reaction.

Alain Johannes: "Back in junior high school, Hillel Slovak and Jack Irons had just started playing instruments. I used to see them walking around. They came to school dressed up as Kiss. Jack used to be Gene Simmons, and for some reason he had this big codpiece. And – I don't know what made me do it; I'd never met him before – I just kind of tested it to see if it was really a little armour piece or not. I gave him a quick punch in the crotch… and it hurt. And he's like, 'What the – who are you?!' We started talking, and we became friends. Him and Hillel had just taken up instruments the year before that, but I'd been playing already, since I was four."

The outfit lasted just one gig, played in the school's gym in December 1977, before morphing into Anthym, a more punk-influenced band than the Led Zeppelin/Queen/Kiss-flavoured Chain Reaction. The band rehearsed daily and as the commitment grew Todd Strasman dropped out. Chain Reaction needed a bass player. Enter Michael Balzary.

"We already knew Flea," Alain remembered, "but he played jazz trumpet, he didn't play bass yet. So he came over my house – it was three months before the Gazzarri's [another of LA's infamous rock clubs, now known as Billboard Live] 'Battle of the Bands' – and I said, 'We've got to be good enough in three months, dude!' He came over every day after school and we ran through bass stuff, and three months later, we debuted."

Balzary had blossomed at Fairfax from the shy muso nerd into a shaven-headed non-conformist whose idea of fun was leaping into swimming pools from the roofs of nearby buildings with his cooler-than-you pal Anthony Kiedis. Anthony and Flea were already stars at Fairfax.

Although Flea wasn't actually a bass player, his musical flair made it easy for him to pick it up, and Hillel taught him well. Flea: "Hillel was a huge

loved the band so much they would pretend to be them, miming along in full face-paint for the entertainment of their friends.

Despite an inauspicious start – Kiedis and Flea met while fighting, Flea and Jack Irons met because Flea was being being bullied by Jack, Jack dressed up as Kiss with his mate Hillel Slovak – the inexorable progress towards the forming of a band called the Red Hot Chili Peppers had begun. Hillel soon discovered Jimi Hendrix and graduated from miming influence on my life. Were it not for him I never would have begun to play the bass. I looked up to him, I loved the way his hair fell on his shoulders and the way he slung his guitar around like a cool rock stud. He had a unique way of dressing and thinking and loving life that inspired me."

Flea's jazz background had given him an approach to playing the bass that pushed the band's sound on to an altogether more sophisticated level, and Anthym gelled with Flea on board. Playing gigs around the local schools meant that they had soon developed a following, and it was this kind of guaranteed crowd that was needed to get your first bookings on LA's club circuit. Despite being too young to actually patronize the clubs as customers, Anthym played in several clubs in Hollywood such as the Troubadour and the Whisky, dingy gig venues which, a decade earlier, had been the breeding ground for the LA music scene that had given the world The Doors.

They scrabbled for support slots, anything they could get. One big moment came when they opened for Oingo Boingo, a Los Angeles band often compared to the more successful Devo (a band from Akron who had since relocated in Los Angeles after signing to Warner Bros), who had a considerable local following. Oingo Boingo's Danny Elfman has since gone on to worldwide fame by penning the theme tune to The Simpsons.

When Anthym played live, Anthony would be there to cheer on his mate Flea. He was soon co-opted to read some of his poetry and tell jokes before the band played. For the extroverted former child actor, taking to the stage was easy. He would introduce the band: "Cal Worthington calls them the hottest rockers in LA. Their parents call them crazy and the girls call them all the time. But I call them like I see them and I call them… ANTHYM!" Cal Worthington, incidentally, was a southern Californian car dealer whose cheapskate television adverts – which featured tigers, camels, elephants, alligators, bears and Cal's own dog Spot – appeared constantly on television in California throughout the 1970s.

Anthony's namechecking of such a mainstream character in a rock'n'roll context was evidence of his part-absurdist, part-vaudeville sense of humour that would become so central to the Chili Peppers' style.

By 1980, they had all graduated from Fairfax. Anthony was enrolled at UCLA, Jack Irons and Alain went to Northridge College while Flea and Hillel concentrated on their playing – the four of them determined to keep Anthym going. In 1981, Anthony, Jack and Alain all quit college and Flea was getting itchy feet. In a period of considerable flux for the fortunes of Anthym, Flea quit the band to join successful local punk outfit Fear, who were making records and appearing on television (their appearance on the popular American comedy show Saturday Night Live ended in controversy after producers became horrified by Fear's punk fans slam-dancing through their performance.

Around this time, the remaining members decided to rename Anthym. They chose the name What Is This?!, echoing the reaction of many people who encountered Anthym's high-energy punk-funk madness for the first time.

Flea's stint in Fear didn't last long. Despite the band's admiration for his spectacular playing – his slap style was already in place – it just didn't sit happily with Fear's sound. Flea quit Fear before he was sacked (he was replaced by former Dickies bassist Lorenzo) and then auditioned for Public Image Limited, the band John Lydon (formerly Johnny Rotten) had formed after the demise of the Sex Pistols. Lydon was in the process of moving to Los Angeles, he had just lost his bass player, Jah Wobble, and was looking for a replacement. Flea got the gig, but then turned the band down flat. He had simply used the audition as an opportunity to play with a band he liked.

By 1983, Flea was running out of ideas. His efforts in trying to find the right band for his exceptional talent had stalled. The auditions were fun but getting him nowhere, though he was always up for getting on stage and just simply playing. Then something incredible happened.

The original Chilis' line-up: JACK IRONS; ANTHONY KIEDIS; FLEA and HILLEL SLOVAK.

13

In the summer of 1983 a friend of Anthony Kiedis was booked to play at the Rhythm Lounge. It was a low-key night of arty silliness, so he asked Kiedis, who had just appeared in the low-budget movie *Suburbia*, if he'd like to come along and do a turn, too. Kiedis loved the idea and decided that he'd perform a rap over a Flea bass line. The pair recruited Hillel Slovak and Jack Irons from What Is This?! to flesh the sound out, and from nowhere, they had a band. They called themselves Tony Flow And The Miraculously Majestic Masters Of Mayhem and played for three whole minutes. They had a poem, a bassline, attitude and a headful of LSD, but their barely rehearsed dynamic fusion of rock and rap, funk and punk astounded the gathered LA hipsters and defined what was to become the pre-eminent sound of LA rock. In front of the crowd's eyes, they invented rap metal. It was as if Jimi Hendrix was jamming with Sly Stone, with the energy of the Sex Pistols and the urgency of New York rap, yet it was immediately recognizable as an LA sound. And

"Get Up And Jump". But there was one big change this time: the band's name. The crowds queuing around the block to experience this exhilarating new band were going to witness the first ever show by a band now called the Red Hot Chili Peppers. "We all knew deep in our assholes," said Flea later, "that this was the real deal."

The new band were going places fast and they needed new songs. They'd been booked for the opening night of a prestigious new rock club called The Mix, a 3,000-capacity venue with Run DMC headlining and Fishbone playing before them. The Red Hot Chili Peppers were bottom of the bill, but despite their lowly position the gig was another triumph.

The Red Hot Chili Peppers were storming the LA scene. But so were What Is This?!, the band that Hillel and Jack were still a part of. Now, the Chili Peppers needed to make the next step. They were playing all over LA, at infamous venues such as the Whisky and strip clubs such as the Kit Kat, where they further sexualized their own already steamy stage act. Egged on by the atmosphere and by a desire to grab the attention of the girls who cavorted during the band's set, they came up with the idea to play naked, except for socks on their cocks. The gimmick did the trick – it outraged and delighted the crowd in equal measure, and cemented the tribal bonding between the band members that was becoming increasingly important to them. It also gave the band an image they would forever be associated with, and an experience they would never forget.

Anthony Kiedis: "I stepped out and everyone else in the band had their guitars in front of them, and I just had a mike cord. I've looked at the footage that somebody shot, and I can see that I'm on another plateau. You really do step into a state of hypnotic transcendental meditation situation. It's all about freedom. It's like being in heaven for a little while."

There was something about the music that called for excessive behaviour, and the more outlandish the behaviour became, the more frenetic and committed the band appeared on stage. They were caught up in

LA took it to their hearts. "I never intended to be a musician until that," says Anthony. "It was a spontaneous orgasmus musical sensation that hasn't left me ever since."

The club's owner was so impressed that he immediately booked the band to headline the club the following week, and by the time the week rolled around, the buzz about this new band had become so great that the club was full by the time they took to the stage to play their two songs: "Out In LA" and

FLEA and KIEDIS with socks on their cocks.

an upward spiral of energy, the creation of their own youthful passion, but accelerated by the speed of their ascendance in the LA music scene and, of course, drugs. The band's heroes included William Burroughs, through Anthony's interest in writing, and musical gods such as Jimi Hendrix and Led Zeppelin – drug monsters to a man. With these icons of the alternative culture filling their creative imaginations, it's no surprise that they took to drugs with relish. Illicit substances were an inevitable part of the music scene and had been a constant in Anthony's life since he was a child. More gigs meant more drugs. Simple.

They needed to record and they needed to be heard by some record companies. Prodded by Kiedis' father, recording engineer Mark "Rooster" Richardson went to check the band out and was impressed enough by what he saw to get involved. He recorded a demo of five songs with the band in Bijou Studios. He put the band in touch with a manager, Lindy Goetz, a friend of his, and the demo tape was sent out to record companies.

Just one month later, the Red Hot Chili Peppers signed a seven-album deal with Enigma Records. But there was a small problem. Hillel and Jack were still in another band and there was some strong record company interest in them too. The time had come and Jack and Hillel chose What Is This?!. This was the band with the longer history, they'd been honing it down for years – should they abandon all that, leaving Alain Johannes in the lurch, just for this upstart band they'd got involved with as a kind of fuck-you joke among old school friends?

Anthony was devastated. They had the record deal, but they'd lost the band. It was the first of a trail of disasters that would dog them for years to come. The story of the Red Hot Chili Peppers had so far been one of blessed success: the band forming, debuting and securing a major record deal in the space of six months. Now it started to get a whole lot more difficult.

Flea and Anthony set about trying to find replacements for Hillel and Jack. They didn't have

much time, and they settled on guitarist Jack Sherman and drummer Cliff Martinez. The latter was a friend of Flea's who'd played with Captain Beefheart on the *Ice Cream For Crow* album and arty punk queen Lydia Lunch. Sherman was a session player. Flea and Anthony had very little time to mould these two into Chili Peppers gang members fit to record their debut album. It wasn't just about playing in a band, it was about a way of life. Anthony: "What we originally set out to do was to be complete and utter perpetrators of hardcore, bone-crunching mayhem, sex things from heaven. To try and describe that to another musician, and have it mean something, is nearly impossible unless you've grown up with that person. It was crazy, but when you get a guy in the band you've got to be prepared to embrace him emotionally for years and years. It's very much like being in love and being married. And you have to be willing to accept and tolerate and compromise sometimes."

Jack Sherman's stint in the band was to prove disastrous, both in the short-term and later in the band's career. But in the meantime, there was an album to make, and they had to make a decision as to who should produce it. The idea of hiring a faceless LA studio producer wasn't something that interested Kiedis and Flea. But hiring Andy Gill, the former guitarist of the English post-punk funk experimentalists Gang Of Four, did. It seemed the right thing to do. Flea and Kiedis loved the Gang Of Four and they hoped that having the band's guitarist produce them would give them that idiosyncratic edge they were looking for.

But the sessions didn't run smoothly. Anthony and Flea were trying to recreate the Chili Pepper magic with what were essentially a couple of session musicians who'd been in the band a matter of a few weeks, and an uptight English guy from Leeds.

The sessions were painful, a pitiful fusion of inexperience, culture clash and the sheer bad luck of losing half the band before setting foot inside the studio. "Maybe he was just too English for us," Flea said later of their relationship with Andy Gill. "We

[]The Gang of Four. Andy Gill (third from left) produced *The Red Hot Chili Peppers.* []

knew what we wanted," Flea said, "a raw fucking rocking album." When it became clear that this was failing to materialize, relations between Anthony and Flea and Andy Gill deteriorated. At one point, the Chili Peppers' taste for the scatological was employed in a practical joke played on Gill – they presented him with a pizza box. Inside was a fresh turd. "All he could say was, 'Typical'," remembered Anthony.

Looking back years later, Flea obviously bore no grudges against Andy Gill: "I love the Gang Of Four, their first two records were hugely influential. They are one of the finest bands that England has ever produced and, consciously or subconsciously, they have influenced a lot of things that we write. They had the funk didn't they? Yeah, they had the English, white angst funk happening."

With the album in the can, the final insult came when the record company insisted that it be called *The Red Hot Chili Peppers* and not *True Men Don't Kill Coyotes* as Kiedis had wanted. They were trying so hard, but there was a real danger that the Red Hot Chili Peppers would collapse before they'd really got started.

Despite the fact that the band's first calling card was starting to look like a dud album, the press were in a state of some excitement when it was released in August, 1984. Glenn O'Brien, in the then new American music magazine *Spin*, called them "the greatest rock band in the world", and overlooked the album's obvious shortcomings: "You can tell this by watching them perform, or you can guess by listening to their forceful, natty and sly debut album." The *LA Weekly* was similarly keen: "the Chili Peppers are going to be THE NEXT BIG THING… Eventually you

will succumb to their absolute majesty, their muscle-funky insight, their Rap-A-Long Cassidy brilliance."

Flea and Anthony were certainly ready for the media. Their own enthusiasm for themselves was infectious as they freestyled on the subject of their own talents. Flea: "We're the grandaddy groove gooses and we drink our smooth juices and we're the slidenest, glidenest, movinest, groovinest, hippinest, hoppinest, rockinest, jamminest, slamminest… we're on a mission." It's an early example of the band's approach to interviews: overwhelm the interviewer with Chili Pepper philosophy delivered, like their music, at breakneck speed. Their psychedelic outlook and inspired wordplay kept them from being labelled sexist frat boy bores by the media, although their free-spirited devotion to sex was certainly going to prove a problem as the politically correct 1980s wore on.

The Red Hot Chili Peppers were in serious disarray when they went on the road to promote their debut. A review in the *Washington Post* from a gig supporting General Public in December 1984 gives some indication of how life was for the band outside of their adoring home town: "Opening were Hollywood's Red Hot Chili Peppers, who pumped out an abrasive and nutty brand of funk and rap that eventually turned much of the audience against them. Their choppy funk was enriched by zany dancing, obscenity, squabbles with the audience and Hendrix-style guitar work."

In this poisonous atmosphere – slogging around the USA with what amounted to a fake band, promoting an album they weren't happy with and facing more than a few negative reactions – Jack Sherman's position in the band became untenable. Flea and Anthony couldn't stand him, and the feeling was mutual. There's hint of the tension between Flea and Sherman in one interview they gave to the *LA Weekly* at the time. In an exchange from an interview during which the Chili Peppers were trotting out their usual high-octane blend of bravado and bullshit, Jack Sherman claimed they'd been offered what would have been, at the time, one of the most amazing support slots a band in their position could hope for:

Jack: "We got an offer to open for Van Halen, but we turned it down."

Flea: "BULLSHIT, BULLSHIT, BULLSHIT, BULLSHIT! We didn't turn it down man. We'd die to play with Van Halen. Bullshit."

Sherman just wasn't down with the programme. He wasn't a Chili Pepper. He wasn't Hillel. So as soon as they'd finished their US tour, they sacked him.

Hillel, in the meantime, still playing with Jack Irons in What Is This?!, was having problems of his own. The band had signed a record deal and released an EP called "Squeezed", but Hillel's interest in them was fading, as was his friendship with Alain Johannes. He found himself more attracted to the noise the Red Hot Chili Peppers were making; he was more spiritually in tune with it. He was also becoming more insular because of a new interest in his life that took him away from his bandmates: heroin. Hillel quit What Is This?! in January 1985 and joined the Red Hot Chili Peppers. He had come home, but by now he was an addict. As was Anthony Kiedis. And a band with two heroin users as members is a band headed for trouble.

The Red Hot Chili Peppers

True Men Don't Kill Coyotes

There's quite a shock in store for anyone expecting the Chili Peppers' trademark muscle-heavy funk rock when they slip the band's debut album on. Now coming up to its twentieth anniversary, *The Red Hot Chili Peppers* is an album very much of its time and while there are echoes of what was to come, there's no doubting this was a very different band to the one that would later deliver "Give It Away" or "Aeroplane".

"True Men Don't Kill Coyotes" is a rather thin rattle, with Jack Sherman's jangling guitar dominating an uneven start to the album and while it's true that here, in their genesis, the band don't sound like anyone else, it's also true that few people would want to sound much like them. Their problems with producer Andy Gill are clear from the start.

Baby Appeal

The genesis of rap rock, but an unsteady start – some ideas seem wonderful at the time, but lose a little as the years pass. The Chili Peppers had the energy and

FLEA: wearing customary few clothes.

the drive, but Anthony's rap is a little hard on the ears and the band are struggling to really rock. Flea holds his own with a monolithic bass pulse, but the huge, echoey drums and Anthony's schoolyard rhyme scheme leave the song sounding a little flat.

Buckle Down

"Buckle Down" is a neat reminder that, outside the studio, in the world of 1984 INXS were well on their way to becoming massive. Starting with a synthesized car-crash, the song lays out a pointed, driving groove, but the drums and bass still sound thin. "Don't give up the fight / In life / You've got to buckle down," Anthony chants and while vocals sound tinny the chorus is undeniably funky; the signs of what was to come are definitely there. Cliff Martinez seems overwhelmed at times by the electronic programming going on around him, but the band do nail a groove – a first on this record.

Get Up And Jump

"Get Up And Jump" arrives fully formed and, finally, the Chili Peppers sound happy, like they know what they're doing and they're actually enjoying doing it. While, again, the Eighties production is distracting at times, Jack's guitar stings as it rides Flea's juggling basslines – there's even some Brazilian-sounding drumming to lift the chorus, which Anthony spits out so furiously you can barely make out the words. Slices of fat, Funkadelic-style groovemanship appear – a pointer towards where the band would go next – but the band still sound in a terrible hurry to be somewhere (anywhere) else than where they are.

Why Don't you Love Me

No question, just a statement of fact, but then, would you love someone who insisted on singing in such an affected, infuriating way? The band's acoustic-tinged boogie has a rough charm, but, again, the bursts of synthesized trumpets and general air of wannabe wacky abandon ends up sounding a bit grating.

"My hair's still curly and my eyes are still blue / So why don't you love me like you used to do?" asks Anthony, who has neither curly hair nor blue eyes. Is he talking about Flea?

Green Heaven

The great-grandfather of "The Righteous & The Wicked" from *Blood Sugar Sex Magic*, "Green Heaven" ploughs the same rap-rock furrow the band set up on "Baby Appeal", but this time it all goes right. Sherman's guitar sounds truly deranged and Flea thumps his bass like it's a dangerous enemy. The band sound *dirty* and Anthony finds it in himself to be serious for once as he addresses the world he sees around him. "We got VD, heroin, greed and prostitution / Tension, aggravation, L Ron Hubbard solution? / Not to mention hardcore chemical pollution". The rap pattern may be a little old school and the verse about the wonderfulness of dolphins may be a little cheesy, but the feeling is all there. "Green Heaven" is where the Chilis truly begin and the seed of a whole new genre of music is planted.

Mommy Where's Daddy

A favourite of the band at the time, especially Flea who, in the sleevenotes to the reissued album, says it was probably the best thing the band recorded in all the sessions that year. Based on a slinky, jazz-tinged groove with, for once, genuinely warm accompaniment from Keith Barry's horn arrangement, the track has a easy, well-worn style, but flounders on an unfortunate lyrical theme wherein Anthony plays a father a little more interested in his daughter then perhaps he ought to be. The lyric, "Well let me see now where to begin / A let me start by tucking you in" may not be too bad in itself, but when it's sung in a faux-crooner style in response to a cooing female voice, you do start to wonder what exactly they were driving at. Then you realize exactly what they were driving at. Ouch.

Out In LA

One of the band's earliest songs gets the full, expensive recording studio treatment. It had been one of the demos that had secured the band their deal with EMI America. In fact, "Out In LA" was the first song that Anthony and Flea actually wrote together, and it neatly covers every one of their many obsessions.

Beginning with a down-tuned heavy rock riff it soon reverts to a liquid funk groove as Anthony raps, "This town makes me jump it's got a lot of bad chicks / Well sure it's got some chumps but I still get my kicks" before a burst of bubbling bass solo from Flea. There follows a hip-hop breakdown, a tale of a "sweet young lass", a comedy voice in the chorus and a squalling, banging explosion of guitar from Jack before a shout of "Step out!" brings the whole thing to a close. The band still sound like they should be playing in bars, but the future is undoubtedly a bright one. Their energy, humour and sense of raw danger is all over this track, making it one of the real highlights of their debut.

Police Helicopter

Another track from their early demo, "Police Helicopter" is more of a riff – a chance for the band to nail a groove and ride it for as long as they damn well please – rather than an actual song. Anthony screams the paranoid lyrics – there are only twenty different words in the whole song – "Police helicopter sharkin' through the sky / Police helicopter landin' on my eye" – as Jack, Flea and Cliff form a tight musical circle around him. This was, understandably, an early live favourite.

[]The familiar sight of **FLEA** wearing his bass guitar.[]

You Always Sing

Right at the far end of the Chilis' attempts at the avant-garde, "You Always Sing" finds them grinding out a deeply angular, atonal riff while Anthony snarls, "You always sing / You always sing the / You always sing the same" seven times before the whole thing grinds to a halt after 14 seconds. "Under The Bridge" has nothing to fear from this rare oddity.

Grand Pappy Du Plenty

The only instrumental on the album, and it's a very different Chili Peppers than one suggested by the partying, girl-chasing, dolphin-loving lunatics displayed elsewhere on the record. Presumably recorded in tribute to the English post-punk hero hired to produce their debut, "Grand Pappy Du Plenty" is a dark, dub-inflected instrumental in which echoey drum patterns and frozen-out guitar glissandos kick it with dust-bowl atmospherics and much moody meandering. Completely unlike anything else in their catalogue, "GPDP" is the sound of a band not sure where they are or what they're doing, a band who, consequently, will try anything once if they think it will help them on their way.

The Red Hot Chili Peppers reissue bonus tracks...............

Get Up And Jump (Demo)
2:36 first released on *Out In LA*

Better than the "proper" album version despite the appalling sound quality. The Chili Peppers are bursting with energy – Flea's bass positively leaps out – but most of this would be lost on the album version.

Police Helicopter (Demo)
1:10 first released on *Out In LA*

Almost identical to the album version. A few extra bass squiggles from Flea and a fair amount of tape noise are the only additional features.

Out in LA (Demo)
1:54 first released on *Out In LA*

The best recorded effort of the extras. Flea, again, shines above all and it's clear they were asked to change the line "Fuck them all" to "Love them all" for the EMI version, but this still sounds great 20 years on.

Green Heaven (Demo)
3:48 first released on *Out In LA*

Beginning with a heavily treated voice, "Green Heaven" is funkier and less menacing as a demo than as an album track.

What It Is (aka Nina's Song)
4:01 first released on *Out In LA*

The most "demo"-sounding of the demos, this track finds just Flea and an un-mic'd-up Anthony running through the song in what sounds like someone's front room. Nina was German punk rocker Nina Hagen, who had had a relationship with Anthony. A version of the track – featuring Flea and Hillel Slovak – appears on Hagen's album *Fearless*.

[Freaky Styley]

The new, improved Red Hot Chili Peppers were determined to get their next album right. For their first they'd chosen one idol, Andy Gill. For their second they chose another – George Clinton – and at the beginning of 1985 they travelled to Detroit to record at the legendary funkmaster's studio.

Clinton was the circus master of the exuberant 1970s funk explosion that was P-Funk, the umbrella term which covered his two projects, Parliament and Funkadelic. Funkadelic, the psychedelic offshoot /progression from the more straight-down-the-line Parliament, scored a worldwide hit in 1977 with "One Nation Under A Groove". With more than 40 players, including former members of James Brown's backing bands, P-Funk was an academy of funk, but the complicated legal knots of running two bands with separate record deals and with so many people on the payroll proved too much, and as the 1980s dawned, the P-Funk empire had collapsed, with Clinton addicted to freebasing cocaine. However, he managed to quit drugs and rebuild his career, and by the time he agreed to produce the Chili Peppers, he was on top of his game once more and had released the superb *Computer Games*, his first solo album, which proved to be one of the earliest object lessons in the potential of sampling.

The sessions for the Red Hot Chili Peppers' second album went like a dream. Hillel Slovak, talking to the *Chicago Tribune* just after the album, called *Freaky Styley*, came out, was full of praise for George Clinton: "He's really smart. He knows when to say something and when to wait. While we were doing our basic tracks, he had a microphone in the control room and he'd speak into our headphones. We'd start playing, and he'd be going, 'YEAH! YEAH! YEEEEEAH! BRING IT DOWN! YEAH!' You'd be hearing this wild, screeching voice in your headphones. It was that kind of vibe."

For George, it was the first time he'd produced a white band. His thoughts on the recording process of *Freaky Styley* echoed Hillel's: "Them boys is bad! They know how to party. They know how to feed chickens." The sessions went by in a blizzard of partying, with Hillel and Anthony continuing to indulge their burgeoning heroin habits.

The album was released to mixed reviews in America and virtually none in the UK. According to the *New York Times*, if the record had any qualities, they were all down to George Clinton: "He [Clinton] has worked wonders on *Freaky Styley*, giving their sound a fat bass and mid-range and taking advantage of the guitarist Hillel Slovak's adept rhythm and lead work." The reviewer was less generous about Anthony's contributions: "The band's rap conceits frequently make them sound silly; they don't brag more outrageously than leading black rappers, but somehow the effect just isn't the same." In 1985, white people didn't rap. Aerosmith were yet to hook up with Run DMC to make the global mega-hit "Walk This Way", and The Beastie Boys were two years away from releasing their debut album. The Chili Peppers, despite having the endorsement of the mighty and respected George Clinton in their favour, were transgressing unwritten rules about white music and black music, and a lot of critics found it difficult to swallow. One described the album as "shockingly tame" and the band as "merely metallic riffslingers with the urge to syncopate".

Touring after the album didn't necessarily garner them much more critical acclaim, although it was obvious that the American media at least were finding it difficult to ignore the Red Hot Chili Peppers. New York in particular seemed troubled by a white band playing funk and rapping. A live review in the *New York Times* reckoned that "... the beat and snarl add up to a pointless display because the Red Hot Chili Peppers – a white band – blatantly imitate black rap groups, adding a tinge of ugly, self-serving arrogance." Whether the reviewer had a problem with a white band being influenced by rap music, or whether he simply thought rap music to be "ugly" and "arrogant" is unclear, but it was obvious that if the Red Hot Chili Peppers were going to achieve large-scale popularity outside of their fervent fanbase back in Los Angeles, they were going to have to work very hard indeed.

Part of their strategy for broadening their fanbase was a brief tour of Europe. They played at London's Dingwalls venue, on a blues bill supporting Muddy Waters' pianist (they were filling in for George Clinton, who failed to show up).

JACK IRONS; KIEDIS; FLEA and SLOVAK.

"Not only were they out of place," said *NME*, "they were complete dickheads, with a dumb line in incomprehensible jokes about their friends. But, as obnoxious as they seemed, the music was awesome, the fiercest musical combustion I've heard this year." Perhaps the UK press were a little less hung up on race than their American counterparts, but *NME* pinpointed the Chili Peppers' appeal; they acted stupid and they were exciting, a combination that had been popular in the UK since punk. That night, despite the crowd wanting none of them, the Red Hot Chili Peppers played four encores, two of them naked apart from the socks on their cocks, to a roomful of bearded blues aficionados. "This sinister virus they call Freaky Styley must've claimed another 30 or so victims tonight," concluded *NME*.

The Red Hot Chili Peppers spent the rest of the year and part of 1986 on the road. By the end of their gruelling schlep around America and Europe, some nights playing to ecstatic sell-out crowds, others performing in half-empty halls, Cliff Martinez announced he'd had enough and left the band. His timing couldn't have been better. Back in Hollywood, the career of What Is This?! was stalling and Jack Irons, the last of the original Chili Peppers line-up from the magical pre-record deal line-up of the band, wanted out. He got out, and slipped happily into the drummer's stool, recently vacated by Cliff Martinez.

The Red Hot Chili Peppers were back together again. By hiring people to fill the roles played by Hillel and Jack, Anthony and Flea had taken the band as far as they could, and had had a pretty tough time of it. It was a real relief for them to have the old band back together. This was the perfect line-up, the one that had created the original Chili Pepper magic, that had written all the early material in a headrush of excitement back in 1983. They'd been to school with each other, grown up together, and it was this deep bond, which couldn't be replicated with newcomers, that had been lacking before.

But, this being the Red Hot Chili Peppers, it wasn't destined to be plain sailing. Niggling away at the band's confidence was the pressure they were under from the record company, Enigma/EMI-

America. Kiedis complained openly to the *LA Times* about the label's performance. He summed up the relationship in one word: "Conflict". They disagreed over which song should be lifted from *Freaky Styley* as a single and, as a result, Enigma refused to finance a video to promote any single. In an age when MTV was achieving spectacular importance in promoting bands, not financing a video was tantamount to giving up on a band. "They want us to fit in AOR or adult contemporary or pop radio or whatever," said Anthony at the time. "They're pressuring us to write something more accessible, something that fits into a category, and I think we're incapable of doing anything other than what we do exactly."

The label really ought to have known better than to expect the band to fall into line and deliver chart-ready pop like musical salarymen – the Red Hot Chili Peppers weren't that kind of band. According to Anthony, when they first signed to EMI, the band got the impression that they were being kept away from the label's head honchos. "They were a little afraid of introducing us to the president and vice-presidents. We'd show up every now and then and we were the favourites with the secretaries and janitors there, but no-one would introduce us to the bigwigs. They had a big board meeting of their international heads or whatever. They were all sitting around this big giant oak table, they had their briefcases out. Michael and I went into the office right next door and took off all our clothes, including our shoes, and ran into the meeting and did a freaky styley dance and tap-danced across the table and basically put everyone into rigor mortis for about five minutes. They didn't know how to react. They didn't have enough guts to fire us." Talking like that, on the record, was never going to improve relations between the band and the label.

But problems with the record label were nothing when compared to the potentially ruinous tensions within the band itself. Anthony and Hillel's heroin addiction was spiralling out of control, and the pair of them were becoming unreliable. They were fast becoming the kind of smack-addled rock stars who blew their careers at the first hint of success, and Flea was getting desperate. With Jack, an ally respected by Kiedis and Hillel back in the band, Flea hoped the situation could be rescued. But in the boy-gang mentality of a rock group on the rise, confessing that you had a problem with drugs was not the done thing. It's part of the pathology of addiction to deny its existence until things have got out of control, some kind of crisis point is reached and the truth and the depth of the problem becomes obvious to everyone. Neither Kiedis nor Slovak would admit that they needed help, and they probably didn't think that they did either. And so the group – and their tensions – continued to rise.

Freaky Styley
Jungle Man

"Jungle Man" – not a version of The Meters' 1974 classic, but a Chili Pepper original – is a vibrant, pounding start to the record. The band appear as a significantly wilder, more dangerous proposition after the rather sterilized appearance of their debut. And there's certainly nothing sterilized about "Jungle Man". Returning immediately to his favourite subject, Anthony kicks off the album with a creation tale in which Mother Earth is impregnated in her "soul hole" by Father Time and a "bare-breasted baby boy" (remind you of anyone?) emerged who went on to "fill the sky with hellfire". "I'm a jungle man," insists Anthony. "I get all the bush I can". No kidding.

Hollywood (Africa)

While the band, worshipping at the feet of another hero – this time George Clinton – certainly sound more warped, the problems do remain. "Jungle Man", for instance, just didn't know how, or when, to stop, whereas "Hollywood (Africa)", a "reimagining" of The Meters' track "Africa", is undeniably funky, but heavily in debt to its creators. It's easy to understand the Chili

Peppers wanting to please and impress Clinton, but very few bands would have the balls to sing, "Take me back / Hold my hand / All the way back / To the brotherland" in front of him. But the Chilis did.

AMERICAN GHOST DANCE

Hip hop was still in its relative infancy when *Freaky Styley* was released in 1985, which goes some way to explaining pieces like "American Ghost Dance". Based on the true history of the Ghost Dance – an attempt by a group of North American Indian tribes to use ritual and ancestor worship to separate themselves from the white men and the religious doctrines they were forcing upon Native Americans – the song is stripped down to bass, drums, a flourish of horns and Anthony's rap. While the track is raw and funky, though, the rhyme patterns and delivery can't help but sound a bit dated 19 years later.

"A new man who is with old ways / He walks the streets of life / But he's in chains / I'm alive he cried," Anthony intones, sounding closer to the proto-rap styles of politicized Seventies acts such as Lightning Rod and The Last Poets than anything most people today would recognize as "rap". "American Ghost Dance" still has a strong and admirable story to tell.

If YOU Want Me TO Stay

"If You Want Me To Stay" was written by Sly Stone, probably the greatest – and possibly the most troubled – blender of funk and rock that music's ever known. His version, written in 1973 for his *Fresh!* album, came about at a time when the Texan musician was deeply involved with hard drugs and many people have put forward the theory that the song was directed (angrily) at fans who wanted him to change his wild ways ("For me to stay here / I've got to be me"). Not much chance of the Chilis doing that during the *Freaky…* sessions, but their version is a tight and neat tribute. Flea's pulsing bass and Cliff's (programmed) drums lock the groove tight while Hillel's guitar layers soft licks and psyched-out noise on top.

Nevermind

Preceded by a drawled burst of jive-heavy pimp rap, "Nevermind" is a great example of how to date your album for all future generations. Consisting of a medium-sized list of all the bands the Chili Peppers are "better than", "Nevermind" manages to sound very Eighties (overblown, cavernous drums and ringing, MTV rock guitars) while dissing such luminaries as Hall & Oates ("a couple of goats"), Soft Cell ("shit / strictly for the twits") and, strangely, Zapp who, through the synth 'n' vocoder work of Roger "More Bounce To The Ounce" Zapp, have gone on to

CLINTON: the Chilis' worshipped at his feet.

Blackeyed Blonde

Set back in the band's beloved location of New Orleans, "Blackeyed Blonde" recalls the manic funk of "Baby Appeal" from their debut and is a powerfully propulsive number – Flea, in particular, threatens the well-being of his own fingers, so furious is his bass-playing, but the production on the track robs it of its weight and leaves only the fury.

The band are stripped of their depth, their bones and their funk. The sense of heaviness they so obviously crave – a heaviness that's all over Clinton's Funkadelic records from the Seventies – is one that the young pretenders can't seem to re-create.

"Blackeyed Blonde" concerns, well, a black-eyed blonde whom eager young men would do well to leave alone. The "black-eyed beauty with the golden crotch / French electric sex a cock shocking swamp fox" has claimed many men in the past, Anthony hollers, before going on to to explain how even renowned lover James Bond met his "Double-0-doomsday" while trying to find "A diamond in the boat". Be warned.

The Brothers Cup

Easily the most successful of *Freaky Styley*'s forays into juicy Seventies funk, "The Brothers Cup" comes complete with a genuinely party-driven groove replete with meaty, sexed-up horns, some gurgling, pre-acid house synths and some of the loudest, loosest drums anywhere on the whole record – but what do lyrics like, "It was our shoulder space / That made the perfect place / For the magic of the cup", mean? In the sleevenotes to 2003's reissue, Flea begins to explain why he had taken to wearing a leather jacket with cups on the shoulders – a look Anthony's clearly mocking on the back cover of their debut LP – but his recollection that, "Anthony and I were deep into being the brothers cup at that point. Anthony invented [the look] when we were in Paris," begs more questions than

be a huge influence on the West Coast rap producers such as, say, Dr Dre, for at least the last 15 years.

Freaky Styley

The title track has an avant-garde flavour reminiscent of "Grand Pappy Du Plenty" from the band's first album. Largely instrumental (the only, bizarrely intonated, lyrics are, "Say it out loud / I'm freaky styley and proud" and "Fuck 'em / Just to see the look on their face"), the track is a moody, heavy-bottomed jam that sadly never really frees itself from its moorings.

it answers, while the lyrics, "We are the brothers cup / We like to get it up", are the usual, early Chili Peppers doggerel. The truth of the matter lies in the lack of apostrophe. Anthony and Flea were the brothers Cup – or the Cup brothers – friends who liked to wear tin cups on their shoulders. Nonsensical? Sure. Get used to it.

Battle ship

A blast of punk rock fury in among the funk and a chance for Hillel to wheel out the effects pedals and make his guitar sound like an angry bull-elephant seal. Another chance for the Chili Peppers to get to grips with contemporary political issues, "Battleship" concerns the aggressive rise in American troop movements in the Middle East. Sound familiar?

"See the sailor boys / dressed in blue / Cheer the change to / Make the news," Anthony screams over a typically taut and grimacing Peppers groove.

Lovin' And Touchin'

The first of three increasingly explicit songs that edge the album towards its close, "Lovin' And Touchin'" sounds like it should break out of its gently thrummed harmonics and blaze forth into a mad, punk-funk break for the border of insanity – but it never does.

A mix of intricately overlaid vocals and Flea's softly timbred bass, the "Loving and kissing", leads to "Rubbing and scrubbing", before "Styling and slumming" almost inevitably provoke an outbreak of "Rolling and cumming".

The romantic flurry of the chorus, in which Anthony promises, "I'll make you my wife and / I'll never forget you" are somewhat undercut by the pungent sniggers that permeate the fade out.

Catholic School Girls Rule

A classic Chili Peppers fantasy track that predates the cop-shagging dream of "Sir Psycho Sexy" by some six years. This time it's the buttoned-up cuties down the local convent who have Anthony all in a flutter. "In the class she's taking notes / Just how deep deep is my throat," he hollers, his excitement rising palpably. "Catholic School Girls Rule" also provides a solid base for Hillel to show off his technique. The closest thing to Eighties MTV metal that *Freaky Styley* has to offer, this is, perhaps unsurprisingly, a far from serious song, but has some wonderful, moral majority-baiting lyrics. "But who cares what the good book says / 'Cause now she's taking off her dress". The video was directed by the magnificently named Rick Dude.

Sex Rap

An infamous Red Hot Chili Peppers number for many reasons, not least of which is the truly bizarre production technique, which takes Anthony's vocals and floats them on top of the music, seemingly by chance, as if they were two different records that just happened to be running at the same time.

Kicking off with a rollicking great drum solo from Cliff, "Sex Rap" is neither sexy nor rap so ends up being far weirder than the title gives credit for. As Hillel and Flea attempt to coral the wild animals that claw at their instruments and keep the whole thing under some kind of control, Anthony sloo-ooo-ooows doo-oo-wn and speedsupdramatically in order for the words to (almost) fit. "We are pumpin' that drvin' bad rhythm / To make those pretty little pussy lips schism". Schism? Really? While he does this, Clinton works his way through the effects open to him and overlays the vocals

with odd pitch shifts and tonal drop-outs until you're never quite sure what's going to happen next. Suddenly the track will disappear leaving only a strangulated Hillel solo or some rattling drums before Anthony wades in again with the latest draft of the most insane lyrics he's ever written. "With my thumb I strum her plum / Start to make her orgasm / Tastes a little bit like oozing hot cum". How do they follow that?

Thirty Dirty Birds

They don't. A miniscule joke preserved forever, "Thirty Dirty Birds" actually isn't about sex. It's about birds. Eating worms. And there's no music, just a string of sounds (worm, burp, chirp etc.) woven into a "poem" and read out in a comedy *Noo Yoik* accent. Odd, to say the least.

Yertle The Turtle

Next to "The Brothers Cup", "Yertle The Turtle" is the coolest, funkiest track on the album, with a sympathetic horn accompaniment and a wickedly sly guitar line that snakes its way through the entire song. Sadly, the lyrics, concerning a megalomaniac king turtle who gets all his subjects to stand on each other's backs so he can climb to the top and get a better view, never lead anywhere. Unlike Yertle, we the listener are left forever on ground level, wondering what's happening over the next musical horizon.

2003 Reissue Bonus Tracks.................
Nevermind (Demo)
First released on *Out In LA*

Although it's very close to the final album version, this demo version is rawer and more punky than the album version proper, though the pimp-rap intro is exactly the same. Anthony has rarely sounded more unhinged than on this noisy relic.

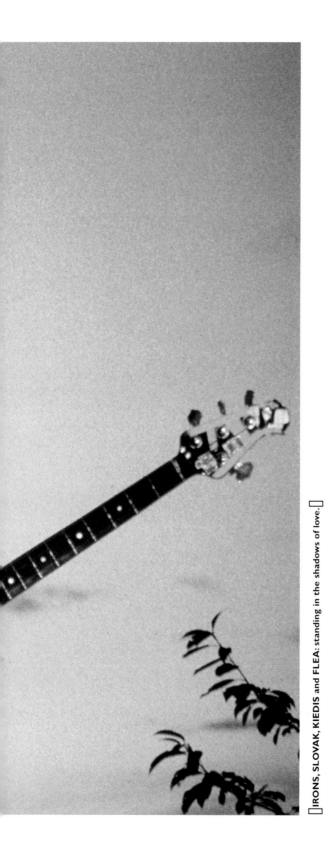

IRONS, SLOVAK, KIEDIS and FLEA: standing in the shadows of love.

Sex Rap

(Demo) First released on *Out In LA*

Almost exactly the same as the album version, just a lot fuzzier and slightly more angular and the lyric, "Tastes a little like oozing hot cum" seemingly began life as "Tastes a little like oozing hot rum". So now you know.

Freaky Styley (Original instrumental long version)

Previously unreleased before the 2003 reissue series, this eight-minute-plus demo is, unlike the album version, completely instrumental and a great deal better for it. A series of increasingly dark twists take the Chili Peppers to places they've never been to before or since. Closer to the motorik grind of prime Can or Neu! than anything else they've ever recorded. A real treat.

Millionaires Against Hunger

Originally the B-side to "Taste The Pain", this "We Are The World" parody probably sounded hilariously biting in 1985, but it just sounds a little spiteful now. Interestingly, Anthony's rhyme style seems to have taken a sudden leap on – he sounds influenced by contemporary New York rappers, particularly Schooly D – but the fact still remains that this is pretty thin fare.

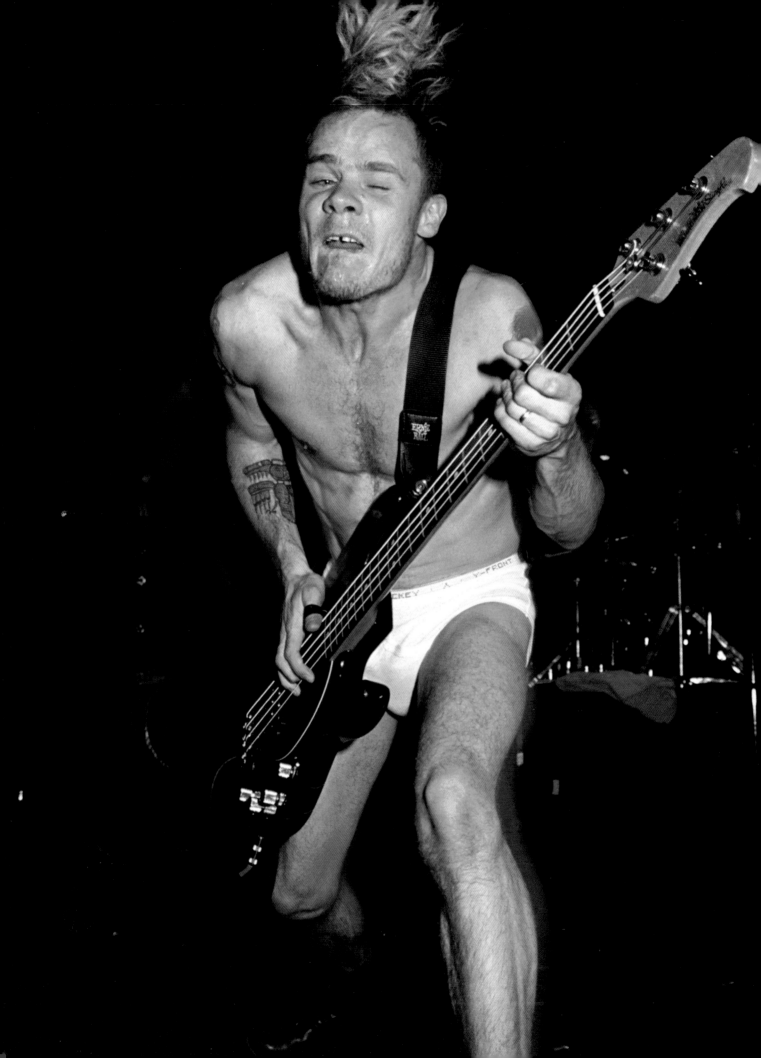

[The Uplift mof0 Party Plan]

In 1986, the band needed to make another album. They instinctively knew that they were still searching for the right producer for what was a crucial role in propelling them on to greater things. Their efforts so far had been acceptable, but they knew they could make better records. They considered somewhere in the region of twenty producers. Even Malcolm McLaren, the former manager of the Sex Pistols, threw his hat in the ring as Flea told *Melody Maker* in March 1988: "He was going, 'Right, 'ere's wot we do. Anthony, you're gonna be the star and you three can sit at the back playing simple rock'n'roll.' That was his concept and we did not wanna go for it. After that he went on for about two hours speeching about how important it is to get back to the roots of rock'n'roll 'cos nothing has ever been done differently, which we don't agree with. He made me faint, man. I fucking fainted. I got real stoned and he just started talking and talking, we were in his room and my head started bobbing and then I fainted."

The meeting with producer Michael Beinhorn went rather better. "We weren't interested in their CVs," said Flea, "just in whether they understood us, and Beinhorn was about the only one who did. We also seemed to get off on the same music, the same rhythms: Jimi Hendrix, Fela Kuti, Stevie Wonder, Sly & The Family Stone."

Beinhorn was a veteran of studio practice. He'd been in the business since the Seventies and although they claimed not be interested, he had the right kind of track record to impress the Chilis. In the late 1970s he'd been in New York Gong with Daevid Allen and Bill Laswell – also a core member of the Golden Palominos – and then gone on to form Material, a studio project, with Laswell and later Fred Frith. Material then produced Herbie Hancock's 1983 album *Future Shock*, which would have impressed the Peppers immensely. Firstly, the album featured the track "Rockit", which, as well as being a monstrous worldwide hit, was one of *the* most important records in the popularizing of hip hop beats and scratching. Secondly, Herbie Hancock, a jazz genius in his own right, was in Miles Davis' legendary 1960s band, and Miles Davis was one of Flea's all-time musical heroes.

As well as these impressive credentials, Beinhorn made the effort to go on tour with the band, to find out what it was that made this group so special. "He came down to New Orleans to spend a few days on the road with us," Anthony told *NME*. "He thought we were one of the best live bands he'd seen, and we thought he was young and hungry." And in the studio Beinhorn's professional detachment from the simmering tensions within the group instilled some objective discipline into the making of a record.

Despite their experience with Andy Gill, the Chilis were open to suggestions from their new producer, and their openness paid dividends. Beinhorn co-wrote one of the album's stand-out tracks, "Behind The Sun". The tune's mellow catchiness was an indication that The Red Hot Chili Peppers were capable of more than just thrashing out

adrenaline-pumped punk funk for frantic crowds of stagedivers out of their heads on booze and drugs. But the Chili Peppers kept their reputation for outrage intact with "Special Secret Song", a title that the record label insisted was used after balking at the original: "Party On Your Pussy".

The band weren't exactly tamed in the studio either. They were still imposing Chili Peppers gang rules, pressing their testicles up against the control room window while Jack tried to record his drum parts for "Fight Like A Brave", for example. "They gave me scrotes while I was playing to give me energy," Jack grinned to *Melody Maker*.

Flea contrasted the experience of recording with Michael Beinhorn to the making of the second album with George Clinton: "Working with George, we spent a lot of time partying," he told the *Chicago Tribune*. "Working with Michael Beinhorn, it was done very efficiently. We worked. Sure, we joked around, but we spent a lot of time in the studio making the album happen. I don't think Michael Beinhorn is better, but the reason I prefer the new record is that George had never seen us play live, and Michael Beinhorn had. And a live performance is such a major part of what we're all about."

Later, Flea elaborated further on why he thought *The Uplift Mofo Party Plan* was more successful than *Freaky Styley*: "*Freaky*... was a great album, but physically it sounds real small now," he told *NME*. "Neither George nor the band were there at the mixdown. We left that in the hands of the mixing engineer, and he sorta lost his erection after we left, and couldn't get it up for the mix."

Another change in the camp was the record label. Whereas they were previously signed to EMI/America (via Enigma), they were now placed with EMI/Manhattan. It might seem like a slender distinction, but in the world of corporate record labels, it meant that the band were dealing with a whole different raft of label personnel – perhaps not such a bad thing considering the animosity that had built up between the band and their former label's hierarchy.

Clockwise from top: KIEDIS, SLOVAK, IRONS and FLEA.

"The new management is much more competent and fun to deal with," said Flea of EMI/Manhattan. "They have a much more sincere appreciation of our music."

The band was advancing. They'd recorded an album they were happy with and the record label had changed and seemed far more supportive. And the album appeared to some positive reviews: "a scorching amalgam of grinding funk, searing metal and scattershot punk" one publication was moved to write. If only the relationships within the band had been so rosy.

Touring to promote *The Uplift Mofo Party Plan* was an arduous experience for the Chili Peppers. Whereas on some nights they'd be playing in sold-out halls, on others they'd be playing to just a handful of the faithful. It was certainly a taxing experience, and a

couple of months into the tour, Flea was feeling the pressure: "On-the-road blues manifests itself in different ways; mainly with us being sick of each other, little things that get on our nerves get magnified by about 50 billion times. It's like being stuck in the same mobile home with eight other people for days at a time. You wind up sticking the gerbil in the fish tank."

And, behind the scenes, Kiedis and Slovak were still using heroin. Flea was deeply troubled. The sex, drugs and rock'n'roll credo was one that he believed in, too. Drugs were fine by him, even heroin – he'd done it himself from time to time. But his bandmates were suffering from drug addiction, and that's very different from high-spirited recreational consumption – although many would argue that one inevitably

leads to the other. The Flea talking to the *Chicago Tribune* from a hotel room in the middle of the *Uplift* tour sounded a very different man to the infectiously enthusiastic freestyler of early interviews:

"We just do our thing. We do the best show we can whether we're playing for ten people or 1,000. We just played to 100 people in a huge snowstorm. And the night before that we played for 1,200 people in Dallas in the sunshine. It doesn't matter, both shows were great." Further into the tour, and his patience was wearing thinner: "We've played 52 shows in 52 different places in the last 58 days. After a while it starts to look like another town, another night and another bunch of drunken assholes." Anthony too was a shell of his former self, described in one interview as speaking in a "whispery monotone".

Talking to *NME* early in 1988, Hillel and Anthony briefly touch on the subject of drugs when quizzed about the hippy symbolism of "Behind The Sun".

Anthony: "That song is based on natural psychedelia, inspired by love and the desire to be at one with people and the animals and the earth, as opposed to LSD psychedelia. Which is not to say we're anti-LSD, 'cos we've all tried it and enjoyed it immensely."

Hillel: "We're all pro-LSD! But drugs are a touchy subject. We've experimented and found some drugs a weeny bit death-orientated."

Flea, in rare moments of down-time, had been keeping himself sane with a little extracurricular acting work. Five years previously he'd appeared in *Suburbia*, a movie directed by Penelope Spheeris, a central character in the development of the LA punk scene. Spheeris' 1981 documentary *The Decline Of Western Civilization* focused on bands such as Fear, The Circle Jerks and Black Flag. Her involvement in the LA punk scene in the late 1970s/early 1980s led to her casting both Flea and Kiedis in several of her later movies, including *Dudes*, which also featured Fear singer Lee Ving.

Three albums into their big-assed major label record deal and the Red Hot Chili Peppers were still in search of a hit themselves. They were still slogging around America's gig treadmill, playing to variable audiences. And every night they demanded of themselves that they perform with as much energy and commitment as ever. *The Uplift Mofo Party Plan* sold respectably, but there was still no hit – no sign that all this hard work was going to pay off in the near future.

With these pressures bearing down on them, it was Hillel who faltered first. His addiction worsened, and his demeanour changed as the band continued on what seemed to be an endless tour. Concerned that Hillel's addiction and his behaviour could jeapordize the band's career, Flea, Jack and Anthony found themselves discussing whether they ought to throw him out and came perilously close to doing so. However, this confrontation of the problems that were being caused by heroin pulled the band back together, and Kiedis and Slovak vowed to kick their habits for an imminent European tour.

It wasn't all bad news. Back in LA, a free lunchtime gig at the Palomino club, sponsored by the radio

HILLEL'S towel was custom-built for decency.

station KROQ, caused a sensation when over 1,000 people were left outside the 264-capacity venue unable to get in. At least 27 carloads of police arrived to try to calm the agitated crowd. "It was a bunch of maniacs getting into a frenzy," said the club's owner, Bill Thomas. "The Red Hot Chili Peppers are hot, but I didn't think they were that hot," he continued. They still had to convince the rest of the world of their worth, but it was nice to know that they could bring the traffic to a standstill in their home town.

In the UK, their efforts were being recognized. The music press, still one of the most important routes to success in the UK in the late 1980s, were sitting up and taking notice. Alarmed by what they perceived as a moribund music biz with a parade of dismal pap filling the charts, the likes of the weekly inkies (*NME*, *Melody Maker* and *Sounds*) and even the monthly style press like *i-D* were on the lookout for bands who might storm the charts

and bring some decent rock attitude back into Britain's pop proceedings. And the Red Hot Chili Peppers were certainly being considered as contenders. They'd impressed many with their energetic live shows and the band, now relatively drug-free, were back on form and filled with a new zeal. In the politically correct Britain of the 1980s, some found the band's sexual appetite and obsessions a little hard to take, but there was no doubt about it: Britain was starting to take the Red Hot Chili Peppers seriously, and their reintroduction of sex into pop music was starting to be celebrated.

Their profile in the UK was upped considerably when "The Abbey Road EP" was released. EMI knocked up the five-track EP around a cover version of Jimi Hendrix's "Fire", which was recorded during the sessions for *Uplift...* and had previously appeared on the B-side of the 12-inch single "Fight Like A Brave". It was a stopgap release, intended to keep new product from the band in the shops while they were on the road. But as it turned out, the EP's cover was to prove more important than the music. What was rather a shoddy EP thrown together from old tracks sitting around in the vaults gave the world perhaps the most recognizable image of the Red Hot Chili Peppers to this day: the four of them striding over the zebra crossing outside the Abbey Road recording studios in St John's Wood – mimicking the iconic Beatles shot taken 20 years previously – naked, save for a sock covering their genitals.

It was a classic image. People who had never heard of the Red Hot Chili Peppers before saw it, and their interest was piqued. People who didn't even like music saw it. Mums and dads saw it. Everyone knew about the Red Hot Chili Peppers. They were the socks-on-cocks band.

The Red Hot Chili Peppers were on the point of mega success. All they needed was to keep it together, and record an album to surpass the last three. What could go wrong?

THE UPLIFT MOFO PARTY PLAN

"*Uplift Mofo Party Plan* is one of the three albums I'd want to take on a desert island with me, along with The Black Crowes' first album and *Smiley Smile* by The Beach Boys." Steven Tyler, Aerosmith

Fight Like A Brave

As far as sheer raw power goes, *The Uplift Mofo Party Plan* is the Chili Peppers at their most virile, most chest-beating, most unashamedly macho. There's an untamed energy here that you can feel the second you put the album on. This is a band in control of their environment. Starting an album with an anti-heroin rant might not seem like the wisest idea ever, but "Fight Like A Brave" is a furiously proud finger raised in defiance – a call to members of the band themselves as well as their fans to resist drugs, to, "Get it through your head / And get it off your chest / Get it out your arm". As Flea recalls in the album's sleevenotes, "Drug use in the band was really beginning to make a morose

[IRONS, SLOVAK, KIEDIS and FLEA.]

stand. It began to seem really ugly to me and was not fun, our communication was not healthy." Sonically similar to The Beastie Boys, with only some nasty Eighties programmed drum noises to spoil the fun, "Fight Like A Brave" is classic Chili Peppers.

Funky Crime

In a nutshell, "Critics say white people shouldn't play funk. The Red Hot Chili Peppers say fuck you." Every white band that have ever played funk, soul or reggae have been accused of stealing other people's music and, frankly, not doing it very well. In the Chili Peppers' defence, they are more than capable of holding down monstrous, water-tight grooves when the mood takes them, and it certainly takes them on "Funky Crime". Hillel's guitar slips and slides all over Jack's rock-solid beats while Flea, perhaps unsurprisingly, holds the whole thing together with some truly inspired bass playing. Anthony, meanwhile, pulls back from the punk and leans more on the raw funk, though he still sounds deranged. Add some liquid vocoder-insanity and it's hip-shake time. "Don't you know funk's colour blind / Well I've committed a funky crime / Against a funky state of mind". That's how it is.

Me And My Friends

To this day a huge anthem at Chili Pepper shows, "Me And My Friends" is the sort of song very few bands could get away with, which is a shame in itself, but one that makes perfect sense in Chiliworld.

A celebration of all things gang-like and rocking, the song starts with a righteous explosion from Flea and never lets up. Nothing else on the album, and indeed few songs in their whole catalogue, matches the sense of bonding and adventure that is captured here. The lines, "It's about my man / And his name is Hillel / For whom my love / Is soul-brother sacred", would become tragically poignant in less than a year, but the guitarist's unhinged solo on the track remains a great tribute to him.

BackWoOds

Inspired by the abortive meeting with Malcolm McLaren, "Backwoods" is the first burst of Chili Pepper sex power on the album. Surely the only funk-metal track to namecheck convicted toilet-watcher and originator of many of the guitar hero poses still in use today, Chuck Berry, the song conjures up the sense of excitement when rock and roll first hit across America and the first wave of black superstars such as Berry, Little Richard and Bo Diddley changed the US music scene forever.

Hillel sets up a loose, swinging groove allowing Flea and Jack to nail a truly dirty groove that erupts halfway through into a sky-scraping solo, ushering in one of Anthony's most graphic sex raps: "A man named Little Richard / Who was born to make them bitches stir / That's right he'll make the sweet substance drip / From the middle of your hillbilly lips". Indeed. On "Backwoods" the Chili Peppers truly found a groove and sound that was all their own.

Skinny SWeAty Man

One of the most frenetic tracks the band ever recorded, "Skinny Sweaty Man", despite being a seemingly throwaway two-minute wonder, is still a regular feature of the Chilis' live set. Flea pulls some truly startling riffs out of his bass, yet he never overpowers Hillel's pungent funk stings – quite a feat at this deadly speed. Could the skinny, sweaty man be a drug-using member of the group? "The caboose that could he goes toot toot," Antony screams, making a throwaway reference to cocaine. "Been known to gag and sometimes puke," he continues. Sounds like Chili Pepper behaviour for sure. Hardcore garage psychedelic funkabilly, as someone with an obvious disorder once noted.

Behind The sUn

Born out of endless hours smoking weed and rehearsing at the EMI studios on Sunset Boulevard in

LA, "Behind The Sun" originated in a Hillel riff that soon developed into an entire song, and one that was quite unlike those that had come before it. Truly a product of the Eighties, "Behind The Sun" had it all – big, booming drums, chiming Simple Minds-style guitars, dolphin references (again!), even a fatally cheesy sitar effect for Hillel's guitar; nothing, but nothing was to be left to chance.

In 1999, Hillel's brother James published a collection of his brother's art and writings entitled *Behind The Sun*.

Subterranean Homesick Blues

Obviously part of the "Bob Dylan invented rap" brotherhood, *The Uplift Mofo Party Plan*'s one and only cover version was Zimmerman's stream-of-consciousness classic from 1965. The most successful cover versions are those that imbue the track with a flavour and meaning that they've never had before, and that's certainly what the Chili Peppers do here.

Ditching all of Dylan's folk-rock colourings, "Subterranean…" sounds new and fresh as Anthony turns the drug-soaked lyrics ("The man in the coon-skin cap in the big pen / Wants eleven dollars: You only got ten") into liquid rap as Hillel, Flea and Jack build a whole new funk base for the song from gloopy bass runs, needle-sharp drums and a strangulated, head-shaking guitar part.

Still a big cherished part of the Chili Peppers' live set, "Subterranean…" proved the band were capable of taking on big challenges and making them work.

Party On Your PuSSy
(formerly Special Secret Song Inside)

When *The Uplift Mofo Party Plan* was first released in the States in December 1987, the album only reached number 148 in the chart. But despite the lowly placing, it wasn't only a small but growing group of devoted fans who were listening. The PMRC, or

Parents Music Resource Center – a group that tried to regulate the music industry by developing the black-and-white "Parental Advisory: Explicit Content" sticker – were tuning in too. Only they weren't really enjoying what they were hearing. In 1985, Tipper "Wife Of Al" Gore and nine other politicians' wives persuaded record companies to warn fans about albums that contained sexual references or lyrics that glorified drug and alcohol use, violence and the occult. Unsurprisingly the Chili Peppers, with songs such as "Sex Rap", "Mommy Where's Daddy" and "Blackeyed Blonde", were getting a lot of attention from those who called themselves the moral majority, and when they heard "Party On Your Pussy" they almost soiled themselves. The album was deemed to be "offensive" and the PMRC insisted all offensive material was cut. As a result, "Party On Your Pussy" was renamed "Special Secret Song Inside" and has remained so to this day.

For all that, there's not much to recommend the song. The living, breathing definition of a one-trick pony, "Party…" is recorded and designed to allow audience participation in its sing-along chorus and once you've heard Anthony grimace his way through, "I want to party on your pussy, baby" once, you've heard it a thousand times. Special extra points for the lyrics, "That girl got a scratch / Slap that cat / Have mercy", though. Frankly, they deserve better.

No ChUmp Love SUCker

True mean-spirited spite doesn't have much of a place in Chiliworld, as their songs are usually much more concerned with sex, dolphins, green politics, sex, being manly and – well – sex. But the bitingly honest "No Chump Love Sucker" is a big thick ball of phlegm right in the eye for some unnamed woman who gone done Anthony wrong.

Over the heaviest punk thrash on this or any other Red Hot Chili Peppers album, Anthony explains how the woman in question was "A bona fide bore / What's more / She snores". So far, so comical, but

The usual suspects – original cast reunited: IRONS, FLEA, SLOVAK and KIEDIS.

there is a dark side to the song – Anthony confesses he lost all his pride when he discovered that all the girl really wanted was "The smack in my bag / And my baseball bat". An easy mistake to make, but one he's unlikely to repeat if the anger on show here is anything to go by.

Walkin' On Down The ROad

An oddly bluesy number, "Walkin' On Down The Road" has a warm, humanist vibe to it, "Groovin' a tune straight out of the womb / 'Cause trust is a must to be a true blue dude", but the song resolutely fails to actually go anywhere. There's another nod to Bob Dylan and a cute verse about a momma bear and her bear cubs, but little else to get excited about.

LoVe TrilOgy

A new type of lyric for a new type of music. Anthony's words were beginning to fly off the paper. On "Love Trilogy" he wrote, "My love can be bigger than / The Hoover Dam / My love can hide behind / A grain of sand", which was undoubtedly the most succinct and distinctive pair of William Blake-inspired couplets he'd ever come up with – if you discount partying on pussies, that is.

Starting off quietly, the track builds and builds and builds from a neo-reggae first verse, through a staggering, instrument-destroying bass solo from Flea before Jack's drums turn from the resolutely funky to the undeniably punky and the whole groove turns dark, twisted and beautifully *nasty*.

"My love for the legs that spread / My love for the fat natty dread" Anthony cries – and who's going to argue with him?

OrganiC Anti-BeAt BoX Band

Recorded live at Capitol Studios in Hollywood in front of an invited audience, "Organic Anti-Beat Box Band" was the Chili Peppers' most pointed stab yet at marking themselves out as utterly different to everyone else. In the form of an extended ballad of their creation ("One comes from the Holy Land / Another was born an Australian" etc. etc.), "Organic…" becomes a slice of truly heroic myth-making. The Chilis and their families came from all over the world, but it was in Hollywood that the band became men, became the *gang* that all great rock and roll groups should be.

As the assembled crowd – including producer Michael Beinhorn and many LA musos – sing their hearts out, a legend is being sealed. The group's last album had flopped; this one would only just scrape into the Top 150, but there is a confidence and a sense of purpose throughout it that goes beyond any concept of success in terms of records sold or hits had. The Chili Peppers were already successful – they were doing exactly what they wanted to do.

"Life is grand in the land of lands / The mind does boggle as the mind expands / The anarchy 4 have manned their craft / Get on your knees and shake that ass". Some things never change.

2003 Reissue Bonus Tracks...............
Behind The Sun (Instrumental demo)
Previously unreleased

Almost identical to the finished version, minus the cheesy sitar and nasty Eighties drums. Flea and Jack work in perfect harmony, allowing Hillel the freedom to experiment to his heart's content. Not much of a song here, if truth be told, but definitely the beginning of something greater.

Me & My Friends (Instrumental demo)
Previously unreleased

Not the two most exciting extra tracks in the series, but this version does allow you the chance to try a little Kiedis karaoke for yourself. As above, very similar to the finished version, but with an added neat, Hendrix-y guitar part from Hillel.

FLEA: during his blurred-head years.

44

⎡Mother's milk⎤

Anthony and Hillel had stayed clean throughout the tour of Europe, but back home in LA they began using heroin again. On June 30, 1988, the unthinkable happened.

The *LA Times*: "Hillel Slovak, 25, guitarist for the flamboyant LA rock band the Red Hot Chili Peppers, was found dead on Monday in his Hollywood apartment. Slovak is survived by his parents and a brother. Funeral services will be held

The results of the autopsy were still inconclusive, but Hillel had clearly died from a heroin overdose. He'd been dead for two or three days by the time he was discovered, and near the body police had found a syringe and a spoon. On the day the band attended their friend's funeral, they had been due to go into the recording studio to start work on their fourth album.

In a revealing news item, the *Melody Maker* reported that Slovak had made no secret of his heroin addiction when the band had been interviewed just a few weeks prior to his death. Talking off the record, he told the paper that his addiction had been causing problems within the band but that he had been making an effort to clean up and was in good spirits. Anthony also confessed that he had only kicked the habit after getting himself in such a state that he was nearly sacked.

"[Hillel] had a heroin problem for a long time and we tried to get him off of it," the band's manager Lindy Goetz told the *LA Times*. "He was doing fine… straight as could be for the last month or so. We thought everything had turned around, but I guess coming home wasn't a good thing for him."

Alain Johannes, who had by now formed a pop duo with Natasha Shneider called Walk The Moon, remembered their early days experimenting with drugs together: "When we were in our early twenties, heroin was a new thing to us and everyone sussed out whether they liked it or not. As time passed, people realized that it didn't contribute to the music and makes your health and mental well-being deteriorate. A lot of people I know have cleaned up. The whole thing of rock'n'roll and drugs is passé. But obviously not passé for everyone."

Flea put it most succinctly: "It's the worse thing that has ever happened to me."

Anthony Kiedis took himself off to Mexico and spent more than a month living in a beach hut where he reassessed his life and tried to quit heroin. On his returned, Flea and Kiedis vowed to continue with the band despite Hillel's death. Jack Irons, however, fell apart. He had been the closest to Hillel, they'd been

innocent schoolkids who dressed up as Kiss together. Jack had left What Is This?! partly because he'd been missing Hillel. And one of the reasons he'd joined the Red Hot Chili Peppers was because Hillel was like a brother to him. Jack couldn't cope with the loss, isolated himself and left the band. He was filled with rage at Slovak's death – he blamed the music industry and wanted nothing more to do with it.

It was rumoured at the time that Jack had quit the band "for dietary reasons", which is quite possibly another way of saying that he was sick of it. He became so depressed that he spent time in a psychiatric ward where, according to legend, he received a phone call from Joe Strummer, the former lead singer of The Clash. Strummer wanted Irons to join his new band, The Mescaleros. "You do know where I am, don't you?" Irons asked. "I'm in my pyjamas in a mental hospital. I haven't played drums in six months." He did join Strummer's band and recorded the album *Earthquake Weather* with him, before rejoining Alain Johannes and recording the debut Eleven album *Awake In A Dream*. While recording the second Eleven album in 1995, Jack was asked to join Pearl Jam.

Meanwhile, Anthony and Flea were in another huge mess. They'd lost their friend and guitarist, and as a result they'd lost their friend and drummer. Ex-Dead Kennedys drummer Darren "DH" Peligro, and former George Clinton guitarist Duane "Blackbyrd" McKnight were drafted in to play an MTV special, but neither were suitable long-term replacements.

After holding auditions, Chad Smith replaced DH Peligro on drums. Finding a guitarist to replace Slovak was going to be a hard task, but the solution turned out to be a rare and sorely needed piece of good fortune for the band.

The son of two musicians, John Frusciante had a natural ability when it came to playing guitar and had already mastered many of his guitar heroes' styles, including the devilishly tricksy playing of Frank Zappa and Jimi Hendrix. His interest in new wave bands such as Devo and The B-52's had led him to punk,

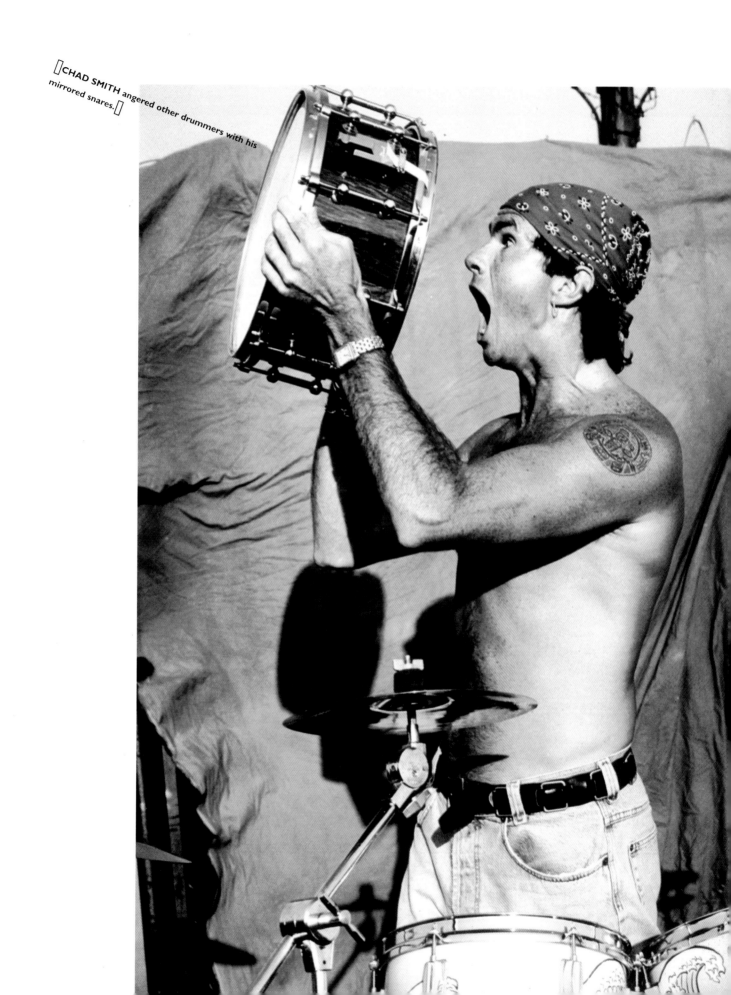

CHAD SMITH angered other drummers with his mirrored snares.

specifically The Germs – the band that inspired him to write his first songs. His talent and hard work was allied to a punk spirit, so when Frusciante first saw the Red Hot Chili Peppers perform a gig at the Variety Arts Center in Los Angeles when he was just 15, he was immediately hooked by what he saw. He was amazed by Hillel Slovak's playing and intoxicated by the band's punk commitment to such an extent that Slovak became the main musical influence on Frusciante and he set about learning every Chili Peppers song.

By the time he was 17, he'd left home and was living in LA. He attended an audition for Frank Zappa's band, only to leave before playing a note. "I realised I wanted to be a rock star, do drugs and get girls, and I wouldn't have been able to do that if I was in Frank Zappa's band," he said. But he was keen to get into a band. Since moving to LA and following the Chili Peppers around on tour, he'd met the band. They knew he played guitar and suggested that he audition for an LA band called Thelonious Monster, who were friends of theirs. Thrilled to have an opportunity to

join a band who were bona fide members of the LA underground scene, Frusciante auditioned. Flea and Anthony were present. His audition proved more than good enough for him to get the Thelonious Monster gig – he was invited to join the Red Hot Chili Peppers instead. Frusciante was just 18 years old, nearly 10 years younger than his new bandmates.

"It was a good thing John came along when he did," Anthony Kieidis said two years later, "Flea and I knew we hadn't accomplished what we set out to accomplish. We had lost sight of the importance and the beauty of what we had created. When John came along he kind of reminded us of the effect we have on people, so it was a shot of fresh, funky young blood right in the face when we needed it."

After a small tour to break in the new members, in 1988 the band were finally ready to enter the studio and record their fourth album, again with Michael Beinhorn in the producer's seat. The sessions were a less happy affair than those for the previous album. Perhaps it was Frusciante's lack of experience, but he and Beinhorn didn't hit it off. The atmosphere in the studio became tense as the band tried and failed to maintain a happy atmosphere in the wake of Hillel's death.

The changes in the band since the recording of *Uplift...* had been monumental, and maybe Flea and Anthony had thrown themselves back into working a little too soon. It was all a bit too much for everyone to take in; the teenaged Frusciante replacing his recently dead guitar hero from his favourite band; Chad Smith having auditioned and got himself into a well-known band because his predecessor had lost his mind with grief; Anthony and Flea having to cope with the death of Hillel and getting to know two new band members. They put pressure on themselves to make an album that Hillel would have been proud of – it was going to be dedicated to him, after all. And Michael Beinhorn had to produce the whole thing. The situation was an emotional tinderbox.

Despite all the raw issues surrounding the band, the resulting album was to prove to be their

breakthrough release. The "Abbey Road EP" had put the band into the public consciousness – that picture of them naked with the socks over their gonads was lurking in the back of people's mind – and the fourth album, *Mother's Milk*, was the one that connected the music to the genitalia for the general public.

Beinhorn's production and the band's more slightly more considered approach to songwriting made *Mother's Milk* their most coherent release to date. Opening with "Good Time Boys", a Chili Pepper manifesto of sorts, the album's standout is a cover version of Stevie Wonder's "Higher Ground". Kiedis boasted outrageously with tongue firmly planted in cheek to *Melody Maker* that Wonder had begged the band to record the song: "He persisted to the point where I'd wake up in the morning and go get my paper and he'd be waiting on my porch. And he went on hunger strike, he got into this serious thing that we either cover the song or he'd commit hari-kiri [sic]. I said, "You can dust yourself Stevie, we're still not gonna do your tune." It finally came down to a financial settlement whereby he bought everyone in the band a Rolls-Royce."

"Higher Ground" proved that, given a decent tune, the Red Hot Chili Peppers could bring their muscular cartoon punk funk right into mainstream radio and on to MTV, and get taken seriously. It seemed they were at their most successful when they explored areas outside the usual amphetamine metal headrush of their punk funk on tracks such as "Taste The Pain". And it was a lesson they were to heed well.

Mother's Milk was released in the UK in August 1989 and had the distinction of being reviewed seriously in many heavyweight newspapers. The *Guardian*, who welcomed the Chili Peppers' injection of a little outrage into popular music, congratulated the band on keeping it together through the upheavals they'd faced and singled out tracks such as "Johnny Hole In The Sky" for praise. UK music paper *Sounds* was impressed, giving it four stars out of five and claiming that the album "has been spiked with an irresistible energy that should leave you dizzy and slightly bewildered."

By the end of the year, the album had sold close to half a million copies in Europe and the USA. It was by far their biggest selling release to date and it gave them their first slew of gold records.

The band hit the road once more to promote it. They played their biggest ever headline show to six thousand people at the Long Beach Arena, California in January 1990.

"Higher Ground" gave the band their first hit. It scraped into the UK singles charts in February 1990, at number 55. The second single, "Taste The Pain", did better, reaching number 29 – a real Top

KIEDIS, IRONS, SLOVAK and FLEA – winter and summer wear.

30 hit. This success spurred EMI to re-release "Higher Ground" in September. It did marginally better on the second time of asking, reaching number 54. To those who were paying attention, it seemed like the Red Hot Chili Peppers were in the charts for months on end.

But still, progress in the UK was frustrating Flea. "It's so humbling for us to come over here," he told *Melody Maker* a few days after playing the Long Beach show. "We're huge in the States, and it's sort of frustrating and confusing that no one knows who we are here."

too much of a painful reminder for him to stay in the band. I think he was unsure whether or not the band would be a breeding ground for future unfortunate experiences. Like maybe he considered that I might die one day and he didn't want to be involved with that.'

MoTHER'S MILK

"Hillel left this plane. He was our dear friend and family, an immense influence on the direction of our lives. We had a blast together. I have beautiful images of him in my head all the time. He showed me what rock music was."

GoOd Time Boys

It takes true courage of your convictions to get over the senseless death of a good friend and colleague and just carry on following your dream. But that's what Anthony and Flea did. With Chad Smith now a full-time member after Jack's departure, the Chili Peppers had every reason to sound a little lost, a little unsure of where they were heading. But, to their credit, they didn't and *Mother's Milk* became the biggest record they'd ever had. It took some bottle to kick off an album following such pain with a track called "Good Time Boys", but the band pulled it off with style.

As the 1990s dawned and the success of *Mother's Milk* became apparent, the band reflected on Hillel's death and drug use in an interview given to *Melody Maker*. Anthony confessed that he had been a "professional drug abuser" in the past, but said that he had been clean for two years. However, his problems with drugs weren't over yet. The band were to suffer more drug-related trauma before they finally rid themselves of heroin.

In the interview, Anthony cited some of Jack Irons' reasons for leaving the band: "I think it was

Tighter and even heavier than on the previous album, "Good Time Boys" revels in its anthemic status and their own gleeful myth-making is clearly evident in lyrics like, "Travel 'round the world getting naked on the stage / Bustin' people out of their everyday cage". Amongst the fury, there's also room for a couple of namechecks – this time it's Eighties funk-metal freaks Fishbone and the band's hero Mike Watt's band, Firehose. "Good Time Boys" is one of the all-time great Chili Pepper tracks. Firehose would reappear in the Chili Peppers' lives two years later when *Blood Sugar Sex Magik* was dedicated to them.

Higher Ground

Stevie Wonder's huge hit from 1973 provided the Chili Peppers with their first really big hit in 1989, but it also provided one of the band's happiest moments in the studio. The band weren't getting along very well with producer Beinhorn any more and to improve the creative mood they invited a giant crowd of friends down to the studio to provide vocals on the chorus. The resulting version manages to be totally different to Wonder's Moog-heavy funk original but to retain every ounce of uplifting positivity. Anthony even managed to squeeze in a tribute to Stevie and a rejection of his own past addictions in his own softly spoken overdubbed last verse, "An' me and Stevie know that, uh, no-body's gonna bring me down / 'Til I reach the highest ground."

Subway To Venus

Humour has always been important to the Red Hot Chili Peppers. They've missed the mark a few times – "Mommy Where's Daddy" springs to mind – but they've never given up on the idea that music can be fun as well as funky, heavy, soulful and affecting. On "Subway To Venus" the old favourite subject of the band themselves and their undoubted prowess in making listeners "wiggle like a wiggley [sic] worm" is given another runabout, but this time the rap-friendly braggadocio is given a cosmic slant. Anthony growls his way through the first verse but settles quickly into a chorus whose chords recall the guitar part from the theme to the infamous Eighties British TV show, *The Young Ones*. Despite being bolstered by one of the brightest horn sections ever to appear on a Chili Peppers record, the track never really takes off, though Anthony's parting shot, "And if I can't make you dance / I guess I'll just have to make you piss your pants", is deserving of a plaudit or two.

Magic Johnson

Born in August 1959, Earvin "Magic" Johnson became a LA Lakers legend during his time at the club between 1979 and 1991. Johnson led the team to five NBA championships (1980, 1982, 1985, 1987, 1988) and became a phenomenon within the world of basketball. Clearly, the Chili Peppers, not shy of showing their love of their adopted home town themselves, wrote "Magic Johnson" as a tribute to the six-foot-nine player and the team he drove to glory again and again.

Over a truly manic, almost militaristic backdrop, the Chili Peppers sound positively deranged as they break

into a series of funk riffs while Anthony spits his way through the the names of other Lakers players (Scott, Worthy, A.C. Green and Seventies hero Kareem Abdul Jabar), but it's Magic that's running the show.

"Lakers are the team that I watch on the telly / 'Cause they've got more moves / Than a bowl of jelly", enthuses Anthony, and who could disagree? In a sad footnote, before the '91–'92 basketball season started, Magic announced that he had tested positive for HIV and was retiring from the NBA though he returned to the club for the '95–'96 season. In October 2003 the Chili Peppers played in the Lakers' old arena. Flea took the opportunity to proclaim that Magic Johnson was the best of all time, even better than Michael Jordan. Later, feeling a little emotional, Flea thanked the audience, saying, "We grew up in this city, we love this city."

Nobody Weird Like Me

One of the first songs that the band wrote with new guitarist John, "Nobody Weird Like Me" dates from the rehearsals the band were having after Hillel's death. As Flea recalls in the sleevenotes to *Mother's Milk*, "My beloved friend D.H. Peligro told me about this kid who plays guitar, he's rockin'. I went over and met John Frusciante and we began to jam. It was a fun time and I think I might have started playing the bass line for 'Nobody Weird Like Me' that day."

Later, John would meet up again with Flea at the bassist's house and they would make a four-track recording of the song together. Flea recalls thinking, "Yeeeeah, this kid's gotta be our new guy." Quite what this new kid thought when confronted with Anthony's lyrics – "Intercourse with a porpoise / Is a dream for me / Hell bent on inventing / A new species" – remains unknown, though the guitarist distinguishes himself here with some crazed improvizations.

Knock Me Down

A new turning for the Chili Peppers, "Knock Me Down" was another anti-drugs song, this time in

tribute to Hillel, wrapped in a newly melodic twist that made it a perfect choice for a single. John would later admit that the track was a "knock-off" of Led Zeppelin's "The Wanton Song" while Anthony's heartfelt words, "Can end up being such a bore / I pray for you most every day / My love's with you now fly away" made no attempt to disguise the pain and hurt for his absent friend. Flea also remembers it as a serious musical change for the band, noting that, "John and Anthony came up with the basis of this song. It was a very important and new creative development those two fostered which brought a new melodic chord change style of song writing to our band which wasn't there before. That John Frusciante knows how to string some chords together."

Taste The Pain

Returning to the pain and loneliness of heroin withdrawal, "Taste The Pain" paints a vivid picture of cold turkey agony. An oddly slinky, reserved track that only lets itself go on a group chorus, "Taste..." features Flea plays some gorgeous cello in support to John's floating harmonics, but Anthony's lyrics leave little to the imagination. "Busted in two / Like a brittle stick / I can not drink / Because my throat constricts / Lovesick from you". Musically, another venture into the unknown for the band...

Stone Cold Bush

... which couldn't really be said for "Stone Cold Bush", a tale of a girl from San Francisco who walked Haight Street with little more than the "skirt on your ass", the lyrics are prime Kiedis: "Sweet china doll her thighs / Her pipes are open wide / She blows more than my mind". The song would be a great deal more forgettable were it not for the incredible bass solo Flea pulls off halfway through, and the ridiculously tight guitar work that both he and John share throughout the whole piece.

JOHN FRUSCIANTE, KIEDIS, FLEA and SMITH: RHCP come last again in the battle of the handsome bands.

Fire

The only song to feature Hillel and Jack on the album, the band's Jimi Hendrix cover "Fire" ended up being a startling tribute to a line-up that could never be reconvened. Though muddier sounding than the rest of the record, "Fire" still comes across as the best last song you could ever hear at a Chili Peppers show. Hillel feeds his guitar through a long, slow phase that lifts his chords and melodies, while Jack drives the song at lunatic speed. It was a brave and commendable decision to place "Fire" on the album – though it would also appear on the "Abbey Road EP" – and one that placed a full stop at the end of one stage of the band's life in a definitive, but still proud way. "Fire" remains a live favourite of both fans and band to this day.

Pretty Little Ditty

The instrumental "Pretty Little Ditty" was written in one of John and Flea's first jam sessions and obviously affected both of them enough for it to be preserved forever as part of the *Mother's Milk* album. In 2000, the central part of the track would reappear as part of the hit song "Butterfly" by the execrable Crazy Town. Describing the process that led to John and Flea being sampled for the later track, mainman Crazy Town said, "I was listening to the Red Hot Chili Peppers album *Mother's Milk* and a song called 'Pretty Little Ditty' was on it. One part in particular hit me as being what 'Butterfly' needed, so I chopped a sample up, put some new drums on it, put a new track to it, and we laid down the vocals. And that was "Butterfly'." So now you know.

Punk Rock Classic

Proper old-school hardcore, "Punk Rock Classic" saw the Chili Peppers taking the piss out of themselves while also having a direct pop at the musical culture that saw anyone who achieved any kind of success as a fraud and a sell-out, a particular bugbear of John's who had been a full-on punk rocker by the age of nine and had been working out his own versions of

songs by hardcore heroes The Germs by the age of 10. Indeed, when John's mother remarried when he was 11 he feared his new stepdad, a philosophy-loving Beethoven fan, might object to his love of punk, but John claims he, "understood where punk rock was coming from. He really supported me and made me feel good about being an artist."

Or, as Anthony would say, "Put us on MTV / All we really need / Begging on our knees / Please, please, please, please, please". And if you still didn't get the message, John threw in a snatch of the riff from Guns N' Roses' own enormous MTV hit, "Sweet Child Of Mine", just to hammer the point home.

Sexy Mexican Maid

Touring. It can do strange things to a man's mind, and it certainly seems to have done strange things to Anthony Kiedis. Written after one too many newly sober and lonely nights in Holiday Inns across America ("Let me please get on my knees I come alone"), "Sexy Mexican Maid" is pure Chili Peppers fantasy, Anthony dreams of awaking to a "Bright and sunny day / So serene she gives to me my toast and marmalade" before the inevitable slide into the profane. This maid it seems, cleans lead singers, as well as rooms, and proceeds to give Anthony a bubble bath where she "tickles me and I laugh / she washes me until I'm clean / Then she does a little sexy dance". Where are these hotels where this happens? How much for a room?

Johnny Kick A Hole In The Sky

Anthony Kiedis has written a lot of insane lyrics in his time, but no one could ever accuse him of not caring about important matters, and "Johnny Kick A Hole In The Sky" concerns itself with the enduring legacy of the persecution of indigenous peoples, in North America and elsewhere. Indeed, Anthony's fascination with the subject, particularly regarding Native Americans, would lead to an enormous Indian totem image created by Henky Penky, a tattooist and friend of the band, that would eventually engulf almost the whole of Anthony's back.

Beginning with an atonal rendition of "The Star Spangled Banner", "Johnny Kick A Hole In The Sky" was a furious burst of anger voiced from the point of view of a Native American raging at his treatment in modern society, "When history books are full of shit / I become the anarchist / I'm pissed / At this". But as the track progresses he gains strength from the spirits of his ancestors and proceeds to create his own magic.

As the last track on the original album it opened the way for the tribalistic, tattooed Chili Peppers that were to reappear two years later on *Blood Sugar Sex Magik*.

2003 Remastered Version Bonus Tracks..............
Song That Made Us What We Are Today (Demo)

Few things separate the men from the boys like hugely extended demo jams, especially ones that run to nearly 13 minutes, so "Song That Made Us What We Are Today" may not be to every Chili Peppers fan's taste, but as a view into what the band sound like when they're left alone to make whatever kind of noise they like, it's unparalleled. And what kind of noise do they like to make? Heavier, more grinding, more intense, completely instrumental, solo-ridden rhythmic metal. That's what.

Knock Me Down

A longer version than the one that appeared on the finished *Mother's Milk* , featuring a lot more of backing vocalist Vicki Calhoun and a whole other rendition of the chorus. Other than that it's exactly the same as the album track.

Sexy Mexican Maid (Demo)

You could barely get a hair between these two versions, though John's guitar is louder here, especially in an arcing, Hendrix-y solo.

KIEDIS: tattoo you.

Salute To Kareem (Demo with guitar track)

In essence an instrumental demo of "Magic Johnson", this tips its hat to Kareem Abdul-Jabbar, born Lewis Alcindor, basketball's most decorated player. After moving to the LA Lakers, he helped them win their five NBA championships. In a musical footnote, Flea and John throw in a manically sped-up version of Black Sabbath's "Iron Man".

Castles Made Of Sand

Live in Cleveland, this 1989 version of the Hendrix classic was previously on the *Out In LA* compilation.

Crosstown Traffic

More Hendrix from the same show, as frenetic as the other was soporific. Reasonable, but not a must-have.

Blood Sugar Sex Magik

For the time being, all was well in the Chili Peppers' camp. The new members were working out, with Frusciante in particular bringing something fresh to the band, they were selling more and more records and playing bigger shows. Flea was a proud father ("I had a baby last year and I've been drinking a lot of breast milk from my wife's tit," he told *NME* when asked why the album had been called "Mother's Milk", and on the surface, it appeared that the band members were healthy, positive and drug-free. Their blend of metal, rap and funk had proved to be a winning formula that had been further adapted by bands such as San Francisco's Faith No More and another LA outfit, art rockers Jane's Addiction. Whereas the Chilis had once been derided for being old hat, trying to bring the sound of the 1970s into the 1980s, or for being a white band playing black music, they were now heralded as pioneers. Perhaps now they could get on with the business of being in a band and finally fulfil their potential.

The next controversies to rock the boat were small beer compared to the level of catastrophe they had become accustomed to. On March 16, 1990, the Red Hot Chili Peppers were playing a gig at Daytona Beach, Florida. The second of a three-night stand for the group, it was being filmed by MTV before a "spring break" audience – a student crowd on a traditional annual knees-up at the beach, usually attended by a great deal of drinking, horseplay and public nudity. For the testosterone-pumping Chili Peppers, it was all too much.

The band had whipped themselves up into an on-stage frenzy of destruction, smashing up their equipment in a time-honoured celebration of rock'n'roll rebellion initially made famous by The Who. Then Flea and Chad Smith leapt into the audience. Flea grabbed a woman in the audience and put her on his shoulders, while Chad pulled her bathing suit to one side and spanked her bottom. Then Flea and the woman fell down, and Flea "knelt on her legs and yelled profanity at her before she cried for help," according to "authorities".

Flea was charged with battery, disorderly conduct and solicitation to commit an unnatural and lascivious act, while Chad was charged with battery. They were released on bail but the band was dropped from the third night's show (they were replaced by Otis Night and the Days, best known for an appearance in the film National Lampoon's Animal House). Flea and Chad ended up paying fines of $1,000 each, and donating $5,000 to the Volusia County Rape Crisis Center.

Meanwhile, the band had some negotiating to do. It was time to sign a new record deal. They were seriously hot property by now. An indication of their mainstream acceptance came when an old B-side, "Show Me Your Soul" (it had featured on the 10-inch and 12-inch releases of "Taste The Pain") had been included on the soundtrack to the smash 1990 film Pretty Woman. Virgin, Geffen and MCA were all interested and Epic Records waded in with a rumoured $5.7 million deal for three albums, but they had the band snatched from under their noses

by Warner Brothers. "At the very last minute," said Kiedis, "it just dawned on us that it might be worth taking a little less money to go with a West Coast company that we really believed in." Warners was the label that had developed respected alternative acts such as REM and had big-selling albums with Peppers contemporaries Faith No More and Jane's Addiction.

"I think the reason we signed them," said Warner Brothers head honcho Lenny Waronker, "outside of your normal record company greed, really has to do with the future – the future in terms of a band that really has a musical point of view and a tremendous amount of strength that has reached a certain level. You can just tell they have all the intangibles.

"We all want the success factor, in terms of commerciality, but the other thing with long-term careers has to do with credibility and the aesthetic of what a band is up to. When you have both those things going for you, I think those are the best bets you can have."

Warner Brothers were showing a lot of faith in the Red Hot Chili Peppers. It was intended as a long-term deal. The record label were trusting that no one else in the band was going to kill themselves with drugs, and they were banking that the Red Hot Chili Peppers were capable of recording albums that would sell a very great many copies indeed. Half a million, the amount that Mother's Milk shifted in its first six months, isn't bad, but it's not enough. To understand how a "$5.7 million" record contract works, it should be understood that the band don't get $5.7 million dollars when they deliver the master tapes of an album to the record company. The $5.7 million is spread over a number of albums, and the record company would have to pay more for each successive album, until the total amount of advances paid comes to $5.7 million and a new deal for further albums has to be negotiated (or the band signs to a rival label). But for the band to get their hands on the bigger advances for subsequent albums, the record label needs to decide whether they want to keep the band on the label. The label has to "pick up the option" – and it's always in the record company's favour. So if a group signs a big record deal, gets paid a million dollars and the album sells badly, the record company can – and often will – drop the band, cutting its losses.

Whether the Red Hot Chili Peppers were fully aware of this when they started the recording of their fifth album, *Blood Sugar Sex Magik*, is unclear. But there's no doubt that everyone knew that this album had to outperform everything they had recorded before. If they were going to make the leap into the big league and keep their huge record contract, this record had to be the creative and commercial success that previous efforts had only hinted at. A duff album at this stage could finish their career.

The producer chosen for the album was New Yorker Rick Rubin. Rubin, a heavy metal fan with an enormous beard and a pair of sunglasses permanently on his face, founded Def Jam Records in 1984 and had produced huge selling and immensely important albums by Run DMC and The Beastie Boys in 1986, two albums that are now widely recognized to have broken hip hop worldwide. And in the following year he produced another Def Jam artist's debut album, Public Enemy's awesome *Yo! Bum Rush The Show*. Rubin's other, perhaps more abiding love was for rock music. He had also produced extreme metal merchants Slayer and The Cult's biggest album, *Electric*.

Anthony wasn't convinced he was the right man for the job. "What he's done before, stuff like Slayer and Danzig, that's an energy that the Peppers aren't a part of, that darker side… but then I realized that all Rubin did was let those bands be themselves. He made us feel very comfortable."

Rubin took the Red Hot Chili Peppers into a large house in Laurel Canyon, an upmarket suburb in the hills near Los Angeles favoured by movie stars and producers, where he set up an ad-hoc studio. In the relaxed but intensely creative atmosphere, between May and June 1991, the Red Hot Chili Peppers recorded a masterpiece.

The band enjoyed the freedom of the environment, away from the "anal retentive vibrations" of a recording studio, as Anthony put it. It was the ideal place to record what Anthony wanted, perhaps a little ambitiously, to be, "the most beautiful record in the world".

They soon fell into a daily routine of getting up at midday or one, and recording through the rest of the day and night. Anthony, John and Flea stayed at the house, while Chad commuted the twenty minutes to and from his home on his motorbike. According to Kiedis, the house was haunted and "Chad feared the wrath of the ghost and so he never moved in. He's

got a Midwestern fear of spirits." But then again, Kiedis also claimed that the house was where The Beatles first took LSD, which might be true, and that it was also the venue for some hot gay love between Jimi Hendrix and David Frost, which isn't true.

They didn't have any time to waste. There hadn't been a Red Hot Chili Peppers album out in two years, and *Blood Sugar Sex Magik* was on the Warner Brothers release schedule for September. This meant that the band also had to give time to the media while recording, but their occasional intrusions, and the arrival of film director Gus Van Sant to shoot the still images for the album artwork, provided welcome breaks from the rigours of making the album.

Under the watchful eyes of a life-size cardboard cut-out of Anthony's basketball hero, Magic Johnson and a large print of The Beatles crossing Abbey Road, the record came together.

"I recorded all the lead vocals from my bedroom," Kiedis said. "John recorded acoustic guitar tracks from his bedroom. We recorded a Robert Johnson song called 'They're Red Hot' from up on top of the hill behind the house. All of the amplifiers for the bass and guitars were in the basement and they were miked down there. We had an intercom system. In the foyer, where you come in, we had an incredible percussion hoedown – trash cans and hubcaps."

When the recording was finished, John Frusciante looked into the camera that had been capturing the whole process for the Chili Peppers' documentary *Funky Monks* and said, "I have never taken anything so seriously in my life, and I have never been as proud of anything in my life." And Flea summed up the band's position as they wrapped up the recording process: "As long as we stay together, there's no way we're going to fail."

They knew they had recorded the finest album of the band's history, just when they needed to.

The record was received with open arms by the world's music press on its release in September 1991. No lesser authority than *The Times* described it as "a stunner", going on to say that "somewhere in the mix lurks the guiding spirit of Sly and The Family Stone" – high praise indeed. The *Observer* lauded the band as the pioneers of funk metal, and *Melody Maker* declared that they were no longer the sexist stereotypical bozos of the past, but an enlightened bunch of tribalist philosophers who talked about their music as art and in terms of their spiritual connection to one another. Musically, they'd sharpened their funk assault, removing the hectic noise and replacing it with considered melody and power, and they'd recorded a ballad, "Under The Bridge", a snapshot of Anthony's life as a "hardcore junkie" when he found himself shooting heroin with a Mexican street hustler called Mario under a freeway in downtown LA. This was the song that truly crossed over, the one that secretaries and mums could sing along to, the one that would be so radio-friendly that All Saints could score a hit with their version seven years later. The album shot straight into the US charts at number 14, their highest chart position yet.

There were clouds on the horizon, though. Frusciante's fragile persona had undoubtedly had a huge impact on the band and how they related to one another, but there were indications that he lacked the

69

Blood Sugar Sex Magik

SMITH, FRUSCIANTE, KIEDIS and FLEA.

thick skin needed to survive the rigours of the rock'n'roll life. "Three or four times in my life," he told *Melody Maker*, "I've completely lost my mind to the point where I had no relationship with this dimension… and in a bad way, too." The day after giving the interview, John left London, unable to handle any more interviews, leaving Anthony to complete the press trip alone.

With the album doing the business, it was time for the Red Hot Chili Peppers to hit the road again. The US tour kicked off in October, and 1992 saw the band arrive in Europe for a month of shows before they jetted off to Japan. But manager Lindy Goetz's confident prediction that "we'll be working this album for a good solid year" was premature. There was, inevitably, trouble ahead for the Red Hot Chili Peppers.

BLOOD SUGAR SEX MAGIK
Power of Equality

From the first few seconds of "Power Of Equality" it's obvious a huge change has come over the Chili Peppers in the two years since the release of

Mother's Milk. Under the guidance of super-producer Rick Rubin, their sound has toughened up immeasurably and, perhaps for the first time, they sound like a band intent on global conquest on their own terms.

"Power Of Equality" lays out a template for the rest of the up-tempo tracks on the album, with Chad's taut, stinging drums, Flea's acrobatic, tumbling bass line and John's funk-driven guitar looser and richer then ever before. A classic album opener, "Power…" finds Anthony clamouring for justice. "Say what I want / Do What I can / Death to the message / Of the Ku Klux Klan," he spits, an unmistakable fury undercutting his words. The Chili Peppers had always been influenced by hip hop, rap and funk, but it took seven years and five albums for them to find the formula that would move them into the super league. *Blood Sugar Sex Magik* was, in the best possible way, a new beginning for the band

If YOu Have To Ask

Rarely has the phrase "chicken-scratch guitar" been so appropriate – John's muted, pecking pulse of a part recalls soul and funk legends, from New Orleans' The Meters to the Minneapolis high-life sensuality of prime-time Prince. "If You Have To Ask" predates Fun Lovin' Criminals' wise-crackin' Mafia hip hop *shtick* by some four years, but the sensibilities are the same. Rubin has constructed a sonic space for the band to live in and each member fills his corner with style. Flea's bass part jumps between a head-nodding thump and a light-fingered twirl that perfectly matches Anthony's tale of "A wannabe gangster / Thinkin' he's a wiseguy / Rob another bank / He's a sock 'em in the eye guy". But however tough he starts out, Anthony can't help but reveal his feelings further into the song. "Searching for a soul bride / She's my freakette / Soak it up inside / Deeper than a secret". The round of applause John received for his exuberant solo was heartfelt; Rubin left it on the record for all time.

Breaking The Girl

A total change of feel and tempo, "Breaking The Girl" showed a far softer, more bruised side to a band that had, so far, been intent on displaying their defiantly macho side. Over a rising, flute-driven throb, Anthony laid himself completely bare. "She meant you no harm / Think you're so clever / But now you must sever / You're breaking the girl". It's long been rumoured that the girl in question was Sinead O'Connor, but neither party has ever confirmed or denied it.

If you think you hear a Led Zeppelin influence, you're right. Nearly ten years after the album's release, John would admit all: "You know, 'Breaking The Girl' was inspired by that Led Zeppelin song, 'Friends'," he told *Guitar World* magazine. "If you compare what I do on the song to what Jimmy Page does in his song, you'll see the similarity! And then,

of course, Thelonious Monk was a huge influence on the chorus…"

Jazz legends aside, the song's lurching, waltz-time tempo and neat psychedelic touches do mark it out as unique in their work.

Funky Monks

Never one to shy away from an overtly sexual theme, Anthony Kiedis surpasses even himself on the fairly self-explanatory "Funky Monks". Over a tuned-down, molasses-thick tempo throb enlivened by John's angular picking and the chorus's falsetto croon, Kiedis lays it on the line. Again. "Every man has certain needs / Talkin' 'bout them dirty deeds".

At the time, the Chili Peppers were deep into their destructively addictive phase, so there can have been fewer more honest opening lines for a

song written by anyone that year than "There are no monks in my band / There are no saints in this land".

SuCk My Kiss

A massive, worldwide hit in 1992, "Suck My Kiss" was quite clearly called something more straightforward until the band and producer realized what a monster record they could have with just a little self-censorship.

More Led Zeppelin influences surface underneath Anthony's righteous, chest-beating rap, as do those of AC/DC, a band Rubin had long been a fan of and one he had utilized raucously on his previous, early hits for LL Cool J and The Beastie Boys.

One of the most intense tracks on the album, "Suck My Kiss" is also home to John's wildest guitar solo, a burst of splintering, bluesy noise that builds inexorably to the point where it threatens to lever itself off the record completely and go spinning around the room under its own steam.

I Could Have Lied

If "Breaking The Girl" was a surprising change in tempo and feel for the band, then "I Could Have Lied" was the point at which they began to show what they were truly capable of. Beginning with just John's gently plucked acoustic guitar and Anthony's mournful howl, the song is a clear antecedent of "Under The Bridge", the chorus exploding into life in exactly the same way that the band's most famous song does in five songs' time. The lyric, "I could never change / Just what I feel / My face will never show / What is not real" could be taken directly from the better-known song.

Throughout "I Could Have Lied', Anthony's voice sits right on top of the music and is only interrupted by John's ragged-arsed solo which, though studded with fluffed notes and bum chords, is more openly emotional than anything else he plays on the album.

[What a pig!]

MelloWship Slinky in B Major

After barely a pause to take a breath, the band head straight back to it with "Mellowship…", which is a litany of Chili Pepper cool, a direct and wire-tight run through the band's heroes over clipped, bone-heavy funk.

So many pop-culture touchstones are mentioned it's hard to know where to start, but there's boxer Mike Tyson, the James Brown, or, perhaps Hot Butter, track "Popcorn", Charles Schulz's "Peanuts", basketball's LA Lakers and their old stadium, the Fabulous Forum, infamous counterculture comic artist Robert "I'd Rather Be Dead Than Mellow" Williams, Jimi Hendrix's "Purple Haze", UK Two Tone heroes The Specials, legendary Washington DC punk-reggae fusioneers Bad Brains, author Mark Twain, Miles Davis' modal-jazz masterpiece *Kind Of Blue*, writers Charles Bukowski and Truman Capote, jazz pioneers Count Basie and Billie Holiday, actor Robert De Niro – the list goes on and on.

"These are just a few of my favourite things," yelps Anthony at the end. Bearing in mind how many other tracks the band wanted to include on the double album, it's lucky he drew things to a close when he did.

The Righteous & The Wicked

Alongside "The Power Of Equality', "The Righteous & The Wicked" represents the overtly politicized wing of the album. Above a groove that sits somewhere between the buttoned-down, music-hall funk of Ian Dury and the Blockheads and the fired-up rage of a young Gil Scott-Heron, Anthony makes his pleas to God to spare his wayward planet and its destructive, violent inhabitants. "Hear me when I'm calling you / From my knees / I am praying for a better day".

It's heartening to know that while Sting and his hand-wringing cronies welcomed in the Nineties' obsession with rain forests and conservation with endless jazz-flecked warbles, the Chili Peppers still managed to sound like bare-chested, tattooed street-punks when singing lines such as, "Holy mother Earth / Crying into space / Tears on her pretty face / For she has been raped".

The chorus makes reference to Marvin Gaye, whose own plea for sanity in an increasingly manic world came in the form of his *What's Going On* album from 1971 – a record Gaye's label Motown deemed so uncommercial they didn't even want to release it. Thirty-three years later it remains one of Motown's biggest selling items.

Give It Away

"Give It Away", more than anything else save "Under The Bridge', is the tune that defined the Red Hot Chili Peppers in millions of minds. Nearly 14 years on, the amped-up chest-beating rap-rock lyrics, jerky, double-octave-leaping bass line still conjure up the video image of the band, painted silver in the middle of the desert – a video that earned them Best Breakthrough Video in the 1992 MTV awards and the subject of an hilarious parody by Weird Al Yankovic.

The song initially seems to be a partly hidden eulogy to the empathic overtones of Ecstasy use ("What I've got you've got to give it to your daughter / You do a little dance and then you drink a little water"), the chorus's admission that "I can't tell if I'm a king pin or a pauper" would certainly back that up, but in typical Keidis style, any deeper meanings soon get buried under a welter of off-kilter flights of fancy ("No time for the piggies or the hoosegow / Get smart get down with the pow wow" anyone?). Bob Marley appears from nowhere to get lauded as a "poet and prophet" and the person who taught Anthony how to "off it", a rare skill indeed. Towards the end the Ecstasy honeymoon is seemingly revisited: "My mom I love her 'cause she love me", "Feelin' good my brother gonna hug me", as the track is yanked from underneath the band's feet. But the truth is somewhat different. Far from being a hymn to Ecstasy, the track is a rallying call for sobriety from the newly cleaned-up Anthony. At 20 he had had a relationship with singer Nina Hagen, who loved to proclaim that the more she gave away the more she received. When he got sober Anthony says he realized that sobriety revolved around giving something away in order to maintain it.

"This idea of 'give it away' was tornadoing in my head for a while," he told VH1. "When Flea started hitting that bass line, that tornado just came right out of my mouth!"

Blood Sugar Sex Magik

The title track finds Anthony pitching his voice down to a low growl as, perhaps inevitably, he launches into a tale of deep sexual obsession. Recalling the squalling funk rock of Jimi Hendrix – a long-term Chili Peppers icon – the track is one of the darkest moments on the album. Beginning with a throbbing, no-nonsense drum break, "BSSM" pans out across John's Eighties future-pop guitar lines and Flea's brutally minimal bass part in support of Anthony's single-entendre lyrics. "Kissing her virginity / My affinity / I mingle with the Gods / I

mingle with divinity". The title track is the dark heart of the album, the moment where the joking and bravado stop and the unflinching reality begins.

Under The Bridge

Anthony Kiedis: "No one wants to admit they need help from the rest of the world, but in that song, I admit that I'm weak and lonely, but at the same time, optimistic. It's inspired by drug addiction, friendship and loneliness in relationship to the city. When you're using drugs, life is pretty lonely. I got clean, but the loneliness didn't go away. I was driving in my car, feeling that loneliness, and started singing the song to myself. I liked what I was singing, so when I got home I taped part of it and started finishing this poem."

[] FLEA discovers the devil inside. []

The song that changed everything for the Red Hot Chili Peppers was written at the band's shared house high in the Hollywood hills. During rehearsals for the record, the Chili Peppers' new producer Rick Rubin would visit Anthony many times, and the pair would sit on an old Fifties couch and talk about the lyrics he was writing.

"That couch was where I first sang that song," Anthony recalled in an interview with VH1. "Rick convinced me to take the song into rehearsal. I was so nervous that my voice cracked when I tried to sing it. The band listened to every last word with a very intense look on their faces. I was about to say, "We don't have to do this", when they walked over to their instruments and started finding what they wanted to do with that song. It opened a new avenue for us. Suddenly, even more than before, everything was okay under the Red Hot Chili Peppers' umbrella."

The song lifted the band from their large and comfortable cult status into something much, much bigger, yet it is as simple as anything they've ever recorded. An opening arpeggiated guitar figure from John segues seamlessly into a solemn soliloquy for the "city of angels", Anthony's beloved Los Angeles. But this angel has broken wings; this is the city where Anthony nearly killed himself with drugs, the city where his close friend and ex-band mate Hillel *did* kill himself; this is the city where even as he's writing the song, grasping the enormous responsibility of his new sobriety, the dark and lonely world is threatening to throw him off balance again. "At least I have her love / The city who loves me / Lonely as I am / Together we cry". In a genius pop move that secures the song as a fully paid-up member of the All-Time Greats club, a heavenly choir, consisting of John's mother Gail and friends, appears to lift the final chorus to a rare and wonderful place.

In a twist few could have imagined, the track got a whole second wave of notoriety when it was covered, to huge success, by pouting English girl group All Saints in 1998. Perhaps one of the few people who wasn't surprised by the song's versatility was Anthony himself, who had many run-ins with unlikely fans over the years.

"I never thought 'Under The Bridge' was going to be a single," he told VH1. "I was at this party in this airplane hanger and went into the bathroom to take a piss. This tipsy guy with a suit and tie pulled up next to me at the other urinal and started singing 'Under The Bridge' in that howling, drunk-guy style. I thought, 'Wow! How is this possible?' Another time I was walking down the street where I lived. It's a peaceful place with a lot of wildflowers and deer and hawks. This car drives by with music playing way too loud, but it's this guy blasting 'Under The Bridge'! I realized that with this song we as a band weren't just communicating to a small circle of friends in Los Angeles and New York any more. 'Under The Bridge' might not swim with the current, but it's out there – putting something beautiful into a stream that gets a little stagnant at times."

Naked In The Rain

From the sublime to the, well, merely all right. No track was ever going to sound good bumped up against

"Under The Bridge", but "Naked In The Rain" is as close to filler as *BSSM* gets. The Chilis' funk rock gets another trip out to play, but outside of the laughably silly lyrics, "Naked in the rain with a killer whale / I can taste the salt when I lick his tail", there's little of interest here.

ApAche RoSe PeacOck

And if it's silly lyrics you're after, how do "Said that girl who left me silly / She liked the looks of me and my willy" sound? The Chili Peppers could never be accused of taking themselves – or their subject matter – too seriously, but even on classic albums such as *BSSM* any listener will get to the point where they're aware of hearing the same themes addressed in the same way. On a record with "Give It Away", "Funky Monks" and "Suck My Kiss", the addition of "Apache Rose Peacock" seems a little unnecessary. Still, worth a listen for more namechecking – this time the reference is to two New Orleans musical legends separated by around forty years: Louis Armstrong and The Meters.

Greeting Song

No faulting the furious noise of "Greeting Song", which tackles the twin delights of driving through LA with the roof down and old-fashioned womanizing. The ghost of Jimi Hendrix is conjured up again by John's breakneck riffing, but there's little of Flea's bass to be enjoyed, such is the welter of guitars and drums.

My Lovely Man

Another ghost hovers over "My Lovely Man", but this one is a lot newer than Hendrix – the track is dedicated to the memory of Hillel Slovak, the Chili guitarist who had recently lost his battle with heroin and cocaine addiction. While usually this would be the cue for some soft acoustic pondering, the Chilis turn their pain into noise and unleash a torrent of bent-out-of-shape guitars and in-yer-face drums. But don't mistake the clatter and disco-tinged chorus for a lack of soul-searching, for this

cuts deep. "Just in case / You never knew / I miss you slim [Slim?]/ I love you too". Truly touching.

sir Psycho sexy

As penultimate sucker punches go, "Sir Psycho Sexy" is hard to beat. The album is almost over, but instead of taking their collective foot off the pedal, the band pull one of the dirtiest, nastiest, most ludicrously sexed-up moments of their entire recorded output.

Strung out on Flea's filthy growl of a bass line, the Chili Peppers recall ex-producer George Clinton's band Funkadelic – indeed, the whole track sounds like it could have slipped off the back of the Detroit band's 1971 album, *Free Your Mind And Your Ass Will Follow*.

Ostensibly the tale of a man the group used to know, "Sir Psycho Sexy" has become infamous – to the point of being banned and deleted from the album in certain Asian countries – for its explicit lyrics. However, in 2004 these things tend to sound a lot less outrageous and a lot more ridiculous. Lyrics such as, "Deep inside the garden of Eden / Standin' there with my hard-on bleedin'" are more likely to provoke titters of amused disinterest than outright moral panic in these post-Eminem times. Thirteen-year-old boys will love Anthony's story of getting his freak on with a "lady cop" and students of the way rock and funk can coexist without pain will enjoy the panoramic drive of the music, but some of us might just want to hit FF.

And what's Sir Psycho Sexy doing now?

"Sir Psycho Sexy is presently living on the planet Uranus," Anthony told *Rolling Stone* laughingly. "He has a small colony. And a pretty impressive harem."

They're Red Hot

Going all the way back – literally. "They're Red Hot" was written by the legendary Robert Johnson, aka The King Of The Delta Blues. The Chilis' sped-up, percussion-heavy version was recorded live in the Californian night and artfully brings to a close an intense and powerful album.

66

[One Hot Minute]

Blood Sugar Sex Magik was selling like no other Red Hot Chili Peppers album. It had topped a million by the end of 1991 and as the band continued touring into 1992, it was fast approaching the two million mark. They'd toured the USA and Europe and were in Tokyo in the middle of a four-night mini-tour in May when John Frusciante dropped a bombshell: he was leaving the band. They had a show that night, though Frusciante was determined to leave there and then. However, the band talked him into staying for one night, and he flew out of Japan and out of the Red Hot Chili Peppers the next day.

Reports in the press were sketchy. His sudden departure meant that the rest of the tour had to be cancelled – Australia would have to wait until October to see the Red Hot Chili Peppers, although it was reported that the band were in Sydney and were rehearsing with an unnamed guitarist they'd flown out from the US. The try-out didn't go well.

Rolling Stone magazine had to remove Frusciante from the image they were readying for the cover of their June 25 issue, and the magazine hit the news-stands with just Flea, Anthony and Chad posing naked.

The band's American PR man, Bill Bentley tried to explain away the split: "John has had, I don't want to say problems, he's from a different mode. This came from out of the blue. He's never really been in a band with this type of exposure or touring schedule." True enough. John Frusicante hadn't been in any band with any kind of exposure or touring schedule before joining the Red Hot Chili Peppers. John's own reasons for leaving were more specific, though no clearer.

"I had a weird premonition that I should quit immediately after I finished my guitar parts on *Blood Sugar…*," John told *Raw* magazine. "I'd say to myself, 'I know you don't have any reason to, but you've gotta quit the band'. But I couldn't bring myself to do it, because I knew they wouldn't let me." He said he felt like he had "400 ghosts" telling him what to do. This wasn't the first time he'd heard voices – in 2001 he told an interviewer that from as early as he could remember he had known that he was going to be guitarist – "There were voices in my head telling me so," he said.

The problems Frusciante had with being a Chili Pepper were complex. He was, and remains, a deeply sensitive musician. He hero-worshipped Flea and Kiedis as a fan, and he was just 18 when he was accepted into the band of brothers that is the Red Hot Chili Peppers. He was disappointed when Flea and Anthony, eight years his senior, turned out not to be as perfect as a boy fan wants their heroes to be, and that led to friction between the three of them. After a couple of years in the band, playing at being a rock star ("It was everything I wanted"), behaving like a party animal, he found a new consciousness based around playing his instrument. And as his spiritual connection to playing became more important, so being a rock star became something he despised. And the "being a rock star" part of being in a band is at its most distilled when the band is on tour. It became unbearable for him, to the point where he even thought he might die. He had discussed his unhappiness about being in the band with Flea a year before he left, but the conversation had been forgotten.

During his tenure with the band, he had dabbled with heroin. It was an occasional and unremarkable thing to do, but once he left, he embarked on a destructive six-year addiction to heroin and cocaine that very nearly killed him.

Back in the USA, the band needed to find Frusciante's replacement fast. They were booked as the headline act on the Lollapalooza II tour, the huge touring festival that had been the brainchild of Jane's Addiction frontman Perry Farrell. They rehearsed briefly with the Circle Jerks' Zander Schloss and even auditioned Brent Paschke, a fan who travelled from Minneapolis and waited outside Flea's home from eight in the morning until three the following morning. (Brent subsequently formed Spymob, who were briefly signed to Epic Records before being dropped without releasing an album. They were then spotted by N.E.R.D. and became their backing band.)

By July, *Blood Sugar Sex Magik* had been in the US album charts for 41 weeks and shifted 2.7 million copies; "Under The Bridge" was at number two in the US singles charts. They were nominated in eight categories at the MTV Awards and they finally had a new guitarist: Arik Marshall, formerly of the locally well-known Marshall Law and an old friend of the band's. He'd once jammed with Flea at a funk club and they'd kept in touch ever since. Arik was given the job 20 days before the Lollapalooza tour started, and the band rehearsed intensively before taking to the stage at the San Francisco Shoreline Amphitheatre wearing flame-throwing helmets. Soon after the 27-date tour,

KIEDIS: notorious hothead.

Arik was replaced by Jesse Tobias, among rumours of friction between Arik and Kiedis. Tobias, found after an ad was placed in a newspaper, was selected over five thousand hopefuls. He lasted two months before being asked to leave. Tobias went to play with Alanis Morissette before relocating to Australia and forming the band Splendid with his wife. Arik Marshall now plays with Macy Gray and teaches funk guitar at the Silverlake Music Conservatory.

In March 1993, the "curse of guitarist" struck in a new and unexpected way when Jack Sherman, guitar player on the first album, sued the band for "breach of contract, fraud and malpractice". He had seen the band's stellar success since his departure and felt that he deserved more for his stint with them. His lawyers even claimed that he had been "treated with contempt and subjected to continuous verbal abuse and ridicule and even occasional physical abuse" while he had been in the band. The case was dismissed a year later, but the process had been an upsetting one for the Chilis.

On a brighter note, the band appeared in an

Former Jane's Addiction guitarist DAVE NAVARRO joined the Peppers in 1993.

episode of *The Simpsons* in May, "Krusty Gets Cancelled" – a sure sign of rock deification.

So, in the summer of 1993, having limped through a year since the sudden departure of John Frusciante, the Red Hot Chili Peppers were once again without a guitarist. This time, the replacement was former Jane's Addiction's guitarist, the glamorous and louche Dave Navarro. He joined the Peppers in September, 1993. Jane's Addiction had split up, following a troubled few years that had seen them release three albums, the third of which, *Ritual De Lo Habitual*, is a classic rock album. Jane's Addiction were well versed in the seamy side of rock'n'roll, living the sex-and-drugs part of the equation to the full. They were the ultimate sleazy LA rock band, underpinned with an underground consciousness and intelligence that put

them in an entirely different camp to the previous generation of poodle-permed lightweights LA had been famous for. Jane's Addiction had finally split following an onstage fist-fight between Navarro and singer Perry Farrell.

Whether it was wise to have Navarro, once a notorious drug user, join The Red Hot Chili Peppers is a moot point. But it did make sense in many ways. Navarro's guitar playing was a thrilling blend of Led Zeppelin rock, choppy funk and psychedelic slurring; he was from LA; he was already famous and used to the world of a major label rock band. And he had history with the Chili Peppers via Flea, who had played trumpet on Jane's Addiction's 1988 album, *Nothing's Shocking*. Plus, the band had already asked him to consider joining them a year previously, when they

To celebrate Dave joining the band they all went out and bought themselves Harley Davidson motorbikes and started their own gang called the Sensitives. Dave became "Angel", Anthony was "Sweetheart", Chad named himself "Tender" while Flea was "Mr Softy". "We're the gnarliest fuckin' gang," explained Flea, "but we don't want to hurt anybody's feelings."

Dave was happy to have joined the band: "I think that everything that encompasses who I am and who I've been in my life has been brought to this band in an amicable way," he said. "I think that I come from a slightly different place, musically speaking. These guys are percussive and sharp edged, to use an expression that Flea has come up with, and I'm into melodic and ethereal sounds. And I think that the combination has really worked and given birth to something really new."

Many fans regard the next period of the band's career as representing a dark time. Some of that perception is down to the album that eventually came out – it had an introspective quality that was somehow gloomier than the likes of "Under The Bridge". It was also down to the effect of the addition of Dave Navarro's guitar playing to the Chili Peppers style (some fans wrote to Navarro telling him he was "ruining" the band's sound). It was also a post-massive success album; always a difficult proposition for any band.

Dave had been in the band a month when the death of River Phoenix – on October 30, 1993 – dealt Flea a huge blow. River Phoenix and Flea had been good friends, and Flea had been with River at the Viper Room the night he collapsed outside the club. River was 23, and he'd died on a pavement with his limbs twitching in convulsion, after bingeing on heroin and cocaine. When the ambulance came to take River to the hospital, medics trying to revive him, Flea had leaped into the ambulance. He was told to ride in the front with the driver.

Another drug death of a close friend was too much for Flea. He was diagnosed with chronic fatigue syndrome, was ordered by doctors to rest for a year, and

were first struggling to replace John Frusciante. He'd declined because they were about to tour with Lollapalooza – which Dave had done the previous year, and he wasn't in a hurry to repeat the experience – and because if he was going to join the band, he wanted to be involved in the songwriting process and not just playing the band's back catalogue.

Flea filed a report to *Guitar Player* magazine on Navarro's joining the band:

"Hey, I want to tell you about our new guitarist. I mean, our new new guitarist. Yeah, the rumours are true – it's Dave Navarro. I'm so happy about it! I had been really worried about how things were going with the band, but now I feel so good. Dave totally knows where we're coming from, has the capabilities to do everything we need, and brings a whole new dimension to the sound. It felt like a real band from the first second we started jamming."

Good idea, lads...

the band entered into something of an hiatus period.

They returned the following summer, appearing at both Woodstock II in the USA and headlining the Reading Festival in the UK in August. Initially, they hit the stage wearing giant light bulbs on their heads, but these were ditched when the band found they couldn't move about easily when they were wearing them. With a few big dates out of the way, the band went into the studio to record their sixth album, with their eighth guitarist.

The album, *One Hot Minute*, came out in September 1995. Again produced by Rick Rubin, it debuted at number two in the UK charts and at number four in the US charts. It took two months to go platinum, but the critical reaction was decidedly mixed. Fans and critics were heard to ask whether Navarro's guitar playing and song writing really meshed with the Chili Peppers' style. Opinion is still divided, but the album is certainly an important part of the band's evolution. According to the *LA Times*, "the highly publicized addition of former Jane's Addiction guitarist Dave Navarro to the Red Hot Chili Peppers makes the LA quartet's sixth studio album hotly awaited but something of a question mark."

Following the release of *One Hot Minute*, the band toured the world, although some dates were cancelled when Chad broke his wrist playing baseball. They were still touring when the single "Aeroplane" was released in February 1996 (it entered the UK chart at number 11) and remained on the road right up to and including the summer festival season. With the exception of their contribution to the Beavis and Butthead movie soundtrack in November (a cover version of the Ohio Players' 1975 hit "Love Rollercoaster") all went quiet in the Peppers camp, and rumours started circulating that they were splitting up. They began 1997 with an appearance on the *David Letterman Show*, and then there was little activity until they were confirmed as playing the Fuji Rock festival in Japan in August.

On July 13, the first of several misfortunes struck. It was to be the start of a streak of bad luck a mile wide. Just two weeks before the Fuji Rock festival, Anthony smashed up his arm in a motorbike accident when an old lady pulled a sudden U-turn in front of him in Los Angeles. With his arm still in plaster, the band made the trip to Japan to play the festival – just as the country was hit by Typhoon Rosie. The festival

site was in the path of the tornado, and 45 minutes into the Chili Peppers' set, the festival was abandoned as the typhoon started to wreak havoc. Back in America, Chad Smith had a motorbike accident. He overshot a red light on Sunset Boulevard and hit a car. "He's lucky to be alive," said Dave Navarro at the time.

Navarro was said to be unsettled by this run of disaster and all the while the rumours that the band were splitting up had been intensifying. For example, when the drummer of Smashing Pumpkins, Jimmy Chamberlain, quit the band, there were rumours that Chad was going to replace him. Another rumour that had gained considerable currency was that the band were going to announce their split at the Fuji Rock festival. Although both rumours proved to be baseless, they gave some indication as to the level of uncertainty that now seemed to surround the band.

It had been said that Navarro had been mentioning that he wanted to work with Perry Farrell again, but publicly he said it was "unlikely" that they'd get back together. However, there was indeed a brief reunion, with Flea on bass and original Jane's drummer Stephen Perkins. *Kettle Whistle*, a collection of live material, outtakes and demos with four new songs, was released in November and the new-look Jane's Addiction went on a short tour to promote it. Afterwards, Navarro told the press that he now didn't feel like playing the Chili Peppers tour, which was scheduled after the Jane's Addiction dates. The next news to emerge from the Chili Peppers' camp was the cancellation of a tour around Christmas.

Talking to *Alternative Press* early in 1998, Dave denied the obvious connection: "That wasn't the reason they were cancelled. I had just been out with Jane's Addiction and I was tired." He went on to enthuse about the recordings the band had been making: "As for [the new Chili Peppers record], we have some completed stuff. I think some of it – one song in particular – is some of the best stuff the Chili Peppers have done since their inception. Some of it is a little more pop-oriented than we might like, but

it's good. It's the strongest material we've done since I joined. We want to finish it this year." The album never appeared.

Stories had sprung up in the US media over Christmas about Dave using drugs. The story, told by Navarro himself in an interview, was that he had called a rehab centre for help with heroin addiction and that during the conversation he'd used the phone cord as tourniquet in order to shoot up. Navarro later claimed the scene he described was from a semi-fictional documentary-style film that was being made to accompany the *Spread* album (a project with Chad Smith), which was yet to be released.

There was more evidence to suggest Navarro's state of mind was becoming unsettled when it emerged that he had also scrawled "I love you" in blood on singer Fiona Apple's dressing room door at a radio station's Christmas extravaganza (people with biochemical suits were called in to wash it off). Navarro claimed it had been a joke – a typical over-the-edge Navarro joke, sure, but just a joke all the same. But the rumours about his health and his relationship with drugs (he'd been sober for five years) were rife. "Have I used drugs in the last year?" he said, when pressed. "Yes. I'm not going to label it as a relapse."

On April 3, 1998, it was announced that Dave and the Red Hot Chili Peppers had parted company. Anthony was quoted in a press release: "This is a completely mutual parting based on creative differences. We had fun and I love the guy." Navarro's statement was rather more rambling. Later, Chad Smith confessed that the situation was a little different from the way it had been presented publicly – they had told Dave that he was out of the band and Dave had been shocked, asking what it was that he'd done wrong.

After tumbling into his own dark period after the Red Hot Chili Peppers, Dave Navarro has since become a part of the truly reformed Jane's Addiction, who released the successful comeback album *Strays*, in 2003. He even appeared to relish the extensive touring that came with it. For fans of the Red Hot Chili Peppers, the past few years had been a roller coaster. And now, with Dave Navarro's departure, had they reached the end? It looked like this time, it might really all be over.

ONE HOT MINUTE

"The only hope I really have is to make music. And that it gets heard. This album took so much time and struggling and working and exorcism. If they don't like it, that's okay. As long as it's heard."
  Anthony Kiedis 1995

Warped

One Hot Minute launches into the emotionally scarring end of drug addiction from the off and "Warped" is a psychedelic drone of pain – Anthony's long battle with the fall-out from serious drug use inspiring one of the band's darkest moments. "Night craving / Sends me crawling / Beg for mercy / Does it show / A vacancy," he sings, Navarro's guitar climbing down from its towering rage to a soft, arpeggiated flutter. This was quite unlike anything the band had done before; the shock many old fans must have felt upon hearing it is clear.

Aeroplane

Flea has had a long and well-documented interest in both jazz and classical music, and there are echoes of both in "Aeroplane", with its languid guitar runs spooling up against chord patterns so strictly structured they sound, at times, like a string quartet playing deep funk. While Navarro's brooding guitar work never really sits right in the group, he finds a lightness of touch here that allows the whole song to fly in a way that Frusciante, with his dextrous, funk-soaked approach, probably never would have been able to.

  Anthony has explained that "Aeroplane" is a song about, "finding something that gets you closer to God

| NAVARRO – beginning to shed cothes.

in a way. There are times I feel terribly disconnected from people and love and peace in myself and in my heart. Certain songs take me to that feeling of pure joy." In the chorus Anthony sings, "Push her voice inside of me / I'm overcoming gravity", and while it's not entirely clear who the "she" is, he did tell reporters at the time of the album how blown away he'd been by PJ Harvey. Describing her as, "My favourite thing right now", he names her albums *Dry* and *Rid Of Me* as big influences. "I can't stop listening to any of them," he said. "Pure genius."

  Anthony did actually meet Harvey while the band were rehearsing in their Hollywood, studio and she checked into the rehearsal room next door.

  "I could hear her singing in the next room with that beautiful voice," he said. "I was just standing there watching her, and I got caught. I felt like a little boy. It was a special, special moment."

  As the track draws to a close Anthony says, "One note from / The song she wrote / Could fuck me where I lay / Just one note / Could make me choke".

  Is that Harvey he's singing to?

Deep KICk

Around the release of *One Hot Minute* Anthony described "Deep Kick" as "100% uncut energy", but there's a lot more to it than pure propulsion. From the spoken word intro ("It started when we were little kids, free spirits"), the track tells the story of how Anthony and Flea went from kids sleeping in "laundry rooms near snowy mountains", through discovering all LA ("The dirty city") had to offer, to the "vital life juice" wasted while watching themselves and their friends "Chase tails round and round in downward spirals" as their drug dependencies grew. Through it all though, the sense of abandon and adventure is never lost; this is a tale well worth the telling. "We were 15, we met at school," Anthony said at the time. "Me and Flea were both social outcasts, but we found each other and it turned out to be the longest lasting friendship of my life."

For someone who told *Q* magazine, "I hate talking about songs. It takes all the fun out of it, it takes the mystery and the beauty out of it," Anthony lays himself totally bare on "Deep Kick", his voice full of wonder and what the two of them got away with ("Those coppers woke us up / Motherfuckers woke us up / Two young brothers on a hovercraft"), but also coloured with a sadness that only loss and regret can bring. But, as Flea so touchingly croons at the end, "The Butthole Surfers always said it's always better to regret / Something you did / Than something you didn't do".

My FriENds

One of the less effective tracks on the album, "My Friends" never really finds its way out of the circular drone of Navarro's psych-meets-country chord sequence and Anthony's none-more-vague lyrics. A tale of depressed comrades and desperate ex-girlfriends, the track only lifts itself into something above the bleakly everyday with Anthony's closing chorus: "I heard a little girl / And what she said / Was something beautiful / To give your love / No matter what".

Clockwise from top: Smith; Kiedis; Flea and Navarro.

Responding to charges of excessive "sadness" in his music Anthony would say at the time, "Despite the sensitive and dark sadness [of the record], it doesn't leave me with the feeling of being sad. The end result is not sadness, but life after tragedy. Surviving."

Coffee Shop

One of the most bizarre tracks on *One Hot Minute*, "Coffee Shop" tries, unsuccessfully, to marry Dave Navarro's intense guitar barrage with one of Anthony's most oblique lyrics. "Confucius might have been confused / And Buddha might have blown a fuse / I ooze the muse", sounds wonderful, but stripped of Frusciante's tightrope-walking funk balance, the song topples uneasily, only finding a sense of space during Flea's all-too-brief bass solo, the one moment when the track allows any light to shine on its constituent parts. "Meet me at the coffee shop / We can dance like Iggy Pop", is Anthony of old, but his libidinous leer is worryingly absent here.

Pea

Flea's solo moment of glory, consisting purely of the man, his acoustic bass and the briefest of backing vocal interjections from Anthony. "Pea" is simultaneously both a gentle and a vicious retort to homophobia and the bigoted, blinkered views that support and propagate such beliefs.

On hearing the song would be deleted in its entirety from the version of *One Hot Minute* released in Singapore due to its liberal use of some prime cuss words, Anthony told a local reporter: "I don't think the lyrics deserve any censorship. It's very honest. Flea wrote the lyrics and he was angry, but anger can be a very strong emotion to draw inspiration from. It's a very obvious, direct lyric. Anger can be expressed in the guitar and tone. Anger can be found in other ways. As we grow as people, we discover what it is to be elements of the population, to be discriminated against, that kind of pain. It's a tragic feeling: to be discriminated against."

One Big Mob

Rarely has a track been so accurately named. "One Big Mob" is, in feel, closer to the Chilis of old than anything else on the album. Beginning with the chant "I am you are me", the song successfully resurrects the idea of a multi-headed Chili beast that rampages unstoppably past, if not through, everything that gets in its way before Navarro's psych leanings pull the song into a dark well illuminated only by the plaintive cries of James Gabriel Navarro, Dave's little brother, who was just over a year old at the time.

"I recorded his voice on a Dictaphone," Navarro recalled to *Guitar World* magazine. "When that song came up in the studio, I didn't know what to do with that section. If I played a guitar solo, it would be really retro Seventies. Anthony doesn't sing in that spot, and I was banging my head against the wall, trying to come up with something to put there. Then I realized, 'Wow, I have the perfect thing!' I ran home and got that tape of my brother. It seemed to fit the mood perfectly."

Indeed it does, the purity of the baby's cry sitting in sharp contrast to the musical fury and raw tribal drive of the verse, but in total harmony with the look-out-for-each-other feeling of the lyrics. "One two buckle my shoe / Take care of me / 'Cause I might be you".

Walkabout

Lyrically Anthony revisits his love of Native American and Aboriginal culture on the album's mellowest track. "The stingrays must be fat this year / Moving slow in my lowest gear / The didgeridoo original man with a dream / I believe the Aborigine," he sings, in tribute to the ancient Aboriginal custom of Walkabout, in which young men from the tribe would wander out into the bush for long periods of time to commune with their ancestors.

Musically, whatever fans may think of Dave Navarro's time in the Chili Peppers, one thing is certain. He gave his all and he told the truth. Around the time of the album he spoke out against some tracks saying he was unhappy with them, and "Walkabout" was one that was mentioned a lot. Speaking to *Guitar World* magazine Dave said, "The

guitar part in 'Walkabout' is somehow the darkest music I've ever played. It's the exact opposite of how I feel. It's very unusual for me, and somehow it makes me sad."

Lots of people took this to mean he simply didn't like funk – surely a problem for anyone recording with the Chili Peppers. Later Navarro admitted that he didn't listen to funk music, that it didn't "speak" to him, but when he got with the Chili Peppers ("three other guys who I love and feel camaraderie with"), he began to really enjoy playing it.

That much is obvious from his liquid riffs and warm wah-wah chops, which sound full of love. "There have been times when I've laughed out loud at the stuff that I was playing," says the Prince Of Darkness. "I don't know if this makes any sense, but I enjoy dark music." Evidently.

Tearjerker

In its own way as open and honest as "Deep Kick", "Tearjerker" is Anthony's own moment-to-moment reaction on hearing of the suicide of the deeply troubled Nirvana singer, Kurt Cobain. Despite (like "Walkabout" and "One Hot Minute") not being one of Navarro's favourites on the album ("They don't really speak to me, I think that they could have been better"), "Tearjerker" has an undeniable sense of drama about it. The track even starts with a theatrical device, a Brechtian interjection ("Can you turn up the track a little please"), which jerks us from our reveries to remind us that we're listening to *ideas*. It also shows not only how deeply Cobain's death struck Kiedis ("I'm feeling sick now / What the fuck am I / Supposed to do"), but what a huge impact the Nirvana singer had had on many other musicians he'd come into contact with.

Cobain – a long-term heroin user – killed himself with a shotgun blast to the head on April 5, 1994. A harrowing photo taken at the scene shows the singer's legs flat out beneath him ("Left on the floor / Leaving your body"), an image that obviously burnt

itself onto Anthony's mind, but while the singer is remembered fondly ("I liked your whiskers / And the dimple in your chin"), it's Kiedis' brutally honest admission of a secret love lost, a moment of pure fan worship, "You never knew this / But I wanted badly for you / Requite my love", that's most startling. A truly moving moment.

one Hot Minute

When asked by a journalist why *One Hot Minute* had taken so long to record Anthony responded, "We have no deadlines or due dates or expectations of when something should be finished. If it takes ten

years to make a record, then that's how long it takes. There's a natural flow of creative unity and that doesn't happen according to a schedule or a deadline." In actual fact, more than a year to record anything is really only the blink of an eye in Chili time, but it had been four years since *Blood Sugar Sex Magik* and a lot had changed. "One Hot Minute" is an intense track, unlike anything on their previous records and like little else they have recorded since. Starting with a grindingly angular bass figure from Flea, the song has strong echoes of Navarro's old band, Jane's Addiction, especially in the chorus, where Aimee Echo's backing vocals subconsciously mimic JA singer Perry Farrell's falsetto yelp.

Navarro's influence on the music is huge too – the track drops into one of his darkly moody passages before lifting itself into a locked groove that goes on and on and on and on and on until finally releasing itself and the listener. A very, very strange choice for a title track, and one that Navarro himself claims not even to be very fond of.

Falling Into Grace

Classic Anthony, refracted through the fractured prism of *One Hot Minute*. Who but Kiedis could take the heartfelt subject of spiritual enlightenment and, somehow, almost without trying, imbue it with lascivious lines such as, "A million years old / But just a little girl / Vibin' off the gong / Rubbin' on the bowls". That takes some special talent. If this track had appeared on any other album it would have been a priapic funk strut; thanks to *One Hot Minute*'s downer-kick it becomes a molasses-thick stumble through growling vocoders and over-egged guitars. Classic Anthony then, but not really classic Chili Peppers.

Shallow Be Thy Game

The Chili Peppers have never shied away from the spiritual. "We've always been emotionally diverse," Anthony told *Q* on the release of the album. "The longer

that we're alive, the more aware of ourselves we become and that gives us the ability to express ourselves more clearly." On "Shallow Be Thy Game" the band take on Christianity in one of their most savage put-downs. While on *Blood Sugar Sex Magik* Anthony had pilloried religion ("Another southern-fried freak on a crucifix" from "Apache Rose Peacock"), here he brims with righteous anger at how God has been used as a threat by religion to stupefy and control people, "I do not serve / In fear of such a curse," he says, his voice rich with power. In sensing his own following Anthony sees himself as "A threat to your survival / And your control company" and Navarro's guitars back up his words emphatically. Perhaps unsurprisingly, Kiedis finds time in his fury to make a quick dick joke. "I might be a monkey / When it comes to being holy / Fundamental hatred / Get down on your knees and (*blow me?*)".

Transcending

Flea's second track on *One Hot Minute*, "Transcending" is a moodily melodic tale of friendship in which the bass-player's love of a good swear word gets a proper workout. Written in tribute to the actor River Phoenix, "Transcending" is, according to Flea, about "One of the kindest people I ever met in my life. When I think about River I don't think about his death. I don't get sad about it. I think about how incredibly fortunate I was to be friends with a person who looked inside me and saw things that no one else ever saw before. And that song is a respectfully loving song for him."

The song itself is a brutal howl, the bare outlines of a friendship born in noisy bars and clubs painted in a few sharp words. "I called you a hippy," Anthony sings. "You said fuck off / Said your brother's a real punk rocker". But no amount of smart words can betray the pain felt at yet another senseless death to affect the Chilis. "Fuck the magazines / Fuck the green machine / See the human being / In a loving stream".

"All there is in life is honesty and love," Flea told *Q* magazine. "There's nothing else, really, and without those, we simply couldn't exist. It just would be ridiculous."

[CaliforniCation]

While he was out of the band, John Frusciante had reached the very depths of heroin addiction. By 1995, he had lost his teeth. His arms were covered with sores from the constant mainlining of heroin, his hair started to fall out and his fingernails were caked with blood. Even his tattoos were ruined. It was rumoured that he was homeless and bankrupt.

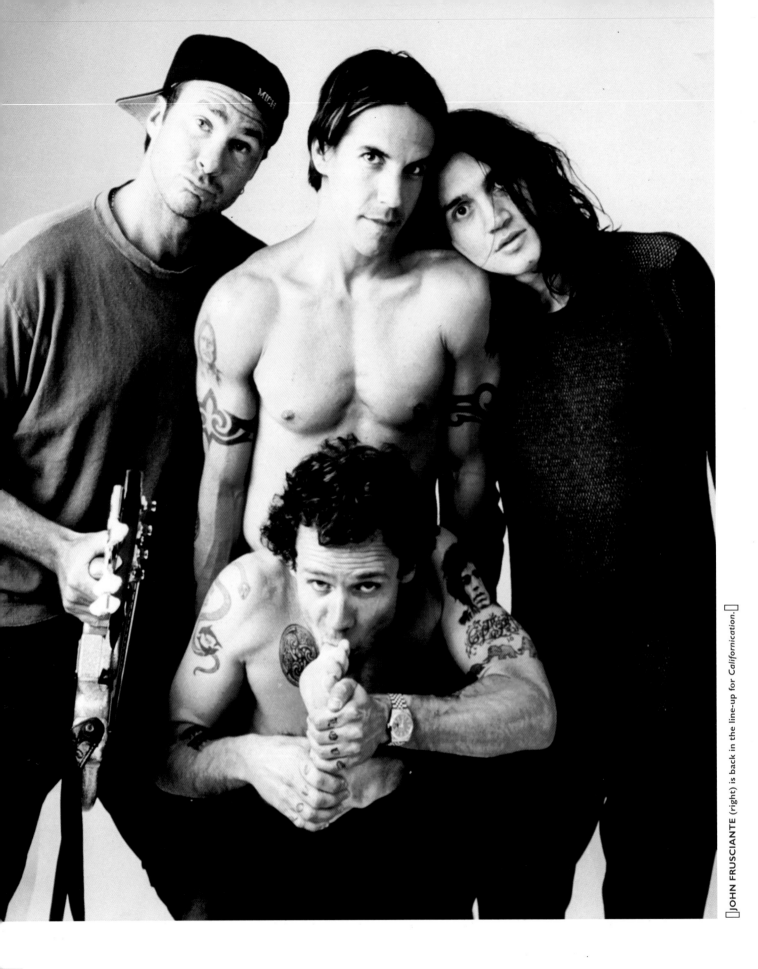

In an interview given to *Kerrang!*'s Ian Fortnam in 2001, Frusciante reveals how his life unravelled after he left the Chili Peppers: "Everything made me miserable, so I made the decision one day that I was gonna be on heroin and cocaine all the time, because when I was on them was the only time I was happy." Nobody could talk him out of it. He communicated with ghosts as his physical health deteriorated, but at the same time he believed that he was doing something that was good for him. He wasn't troubled with guilt about being a junkie. Voices in his head had allowed him six years to be a junkie, and he didn't care whether he lived or died. And he came very close to dying. But, miraculously, when those six years were up, in January 1998, he booked himself into rehab and cleaned up. He figured that he had three months left to live if he continued taking drugs. The voices in his head (his "spirits") had told him to play the guitar when he was a child, they told him to quit the band back in 1992, they told him to take the drugs, and they told him to quit the drugs, too. As always, he obeyed the voices.

Flea had been in fairly regular contact with John through his plunge into drug hell. Anthony had bumped into him once or twice, but it had always been awkward between the two of them. When Anthony and Flea started to feel that things weren't working out with Dave, they had began to wonder whether perhaps this really was the end of the band. The question was being asked, not for the first time, but this time it seemed like there might be no other option. And then Flea asked Anthony how he'd feel to have John back in the band. "That would be a dream come true, but it seems unlikely," was Anthony's response. Flea thought otherwise.

Anthony and Flea met up with John towards the end of 1997. They knew that he was serious about kicking his heroin addiction, and were supporting him. Anthony himself had been in and out of heroin addiction, so he was more than sympathetic. They also knew that they had problems with Dave Navarro and that the real Chili Pepper magic had happened when John was in the band. If only he was healthy, maybe they could re-create it.

Then, one day in April, 1998, Chad received a phone call from Flea. "We're watching the Lakers game, you should come over," he said. Five minutes later, Flea called again, "Anthony's coming as well, so you'd better come, too." Chad suspected something was up and when he sat down, Anthony and Flea told Chad that they wanted to sack Dave and get John back in again. Flea had already asked John if he would rejoin the band, and he'd said yes without hesitation.

And thus John Frusciante rejoined the band. There was some nervousness when he was slightly late for the band's first jam session. Anthony, Flea and Chad were waiting for John in Flea's garage. Would it be OK? They cracked jokes and tried to lighten the atmosphere. Then John opened the door. They greeted one another, John plugged his guitar in and said, "Let's do it." Anthony recalled the moment: "It was like a dead friend… it was like a friend whom I thought I'd never see again suddenly came into the room with a guitar and an amp and said 'Let's do it'. I was very happy to see John playing the guitar and banging his head. The moment the sound came out it was so funky, that I don't think I'll ever experience that feeling ever again. That session was so great."

Frusciante was moved by the experience, too: "It was great. But I had very little technical skill. I'd hardly played my guitar for five years, but the way they took me back made me feel good about myself. It felt so good to have friends who really believed in me when nobody else did, because I was a person who was pretty much thought of as finished."

The rejuvinated band took its first faltering steps into the live arena by playing a secret date on June 12 at the 9:30 Club in Washington DC. The following day they were due to play on the The Beastie Boys' Tibetan Freedom Concert, but severe weather put a stop on the gig, and they ended up playing the following day instead.

The Red Hot Chili Peppers were back and were jamming together to work up material for a new album, as well as playing the odd live date, including a secret show with Garbage supporting in July. They went into the studio, again with Rick Rubin, to record *Californication*. "We went in and worked with Rick for about a month and recorded the whole album in like three weeks," said Chad Smith. It was released in June, 1999, and entered the US album chart at number three.

As far as the media were concerned, the delay of four years between *One Hot Minute* and *Californication* was down to drugs, but Anthony thought differently: "I don't think that drugs are why there was a long wait for the album. I've been to a few rehabs in my life, yes, but I also got a lot of work done in between that time. To me, we started working on this record just a little over a year ago. Those three years prior it was just *life*, you know?"

"Bunting out for Frusciante's return," trumpeted *Q* magazine in their review of *Californication*. "Positively mellow 'Road Tripping' celebrates his joining Kiedis and Flea on a restorative camping trip. Ass intermittently kicked, but no dead horses flogged. The little song 'Porcelain' and 'Savior' reveal new subtlety and even gentleness."

The album's title track was the first one they tried to write when Frusciante first rejoined the band. It took another seven months before they finished it. A melancholy satire of his home state's ability to infiltrate the most faraway places with its commercial output (inspired by Kiedis' travels in Indonesia, where he came across Chili Peppers T-shirts and Gun N' Roses CDs), *Californication* was a mesmerizing shift of gear for the band. The *Guardian* gave the album a positive review, marking Kiedis out for attention: "Anthony Kiedis' drug history may or may not be the source of his voice's throat-catching poignancy, but there's something about him that's for real – a feeling that permeates all corners of the record." New York's *Newsday* said that with Frusciante back on the guitar duties, "the equation is right again" and *NME* described the album as being the sound of the band at their most reflective.

The Chilis were overjoyed with the results of Frusciante's return. Flea said that he thought the band was now "all about John Frusciante. I am honoured to be in a band with him." Chad was equally effusive: "He's an inspiring person, he's amazing. We're in the studio all day, all night, and he goes home and plays guitar to the Ramones' *Rocket To Russia* or something. He learns every little solo on BBC Led Zeppelin records. I went home and slept! He's just all about music and art all day and all night. It's what he lives for."

The summer saw the band play the festivals, including shows at Reading and Leeds in the UK and another Woodstock festival in Rome, NY, in the USA. The latter ended badly when fires lit during the band's set swept out of control and riot police had to be called when elements of the crowd started causing damage. The band's encore was delayed as one of the festival's organizers told the crowd that one of the speaker towers was on fire, and that they needed to make room for a fire engine to get to it. Several trucks near the stage caught fire and one exploded, while some concert-goers continued lighting fires and causing mayhem.

In October, to promote the release of the single "Around The World", the Chili Peppers played on the 107th floor of the World Trade Center, a stunt hosted by the radio station K-Rock, before heading off around the world for a tour that included Europe, Australia and South America, starting in Finland.

Fans who couldn't wait to see their heroes in the flesh could whet their appetites by going to see Flea's latest movie appearance in the independent film *Liar's Poker*. For someone who said simply of his acting career, "I've done a few things that have fallen into my lap", Flea had amassed an impressive track record in the movies, having by now clocked up appearances in *My Own Private Idaho*, *Back To The Future II* and *Back To The Future III*, *Less Than Zero*, *The Big Lebowski* and *Fear And Loathing In Las Vegas*.

In November, 1999, it was announced that *Californication* had gone multi-platinum, having sold two million copies. This success was replicated across the world: In Italy, the album went triple platinum, in Canada and Australia double platinum and platinum in Japan, Denmark and Sweden. It was also reported that Flea had had a pair of pants stolen from his dressing room in Milan. He was desperate to get them back as they had considerable sentimental value for him. We assume this is the American understanding of the word "pants", although with the Chili Peppers, we can never be too sure.

Into 2000, and the band were conquering the world; a sold-out tour in Japan began on January 8 and included a three-night stand at Tokyo's Budokan, where Flea confessed that he was having a few problems with his hearing and started to wear earplugs on stage. "The sheer volume of our rock power was causing me great pain," he said. There was also an incident where he dived into the audience and people started "jumping all over me". He accidentally hit a girl with his bass guitar, so he took her to the side of the stage and gave her his bass. "She was very sweet," Flea said. Next on the tour was Australia and New Zealand for the Big Day Out festival tour.

In April, 2000, the band was touring the USA with the Foo Fighters and Muse supporting, and Flea and Frusciante started working on songs for the next album. Touring was relentless. The third leg of their US trek was coming to an end in early June, and the band were coping. "As a band we are good," said Flea. "It is an emotional test to be at such close quarters with people for such a long period of time. At least we all love each other and shit. We do rock like fucking crazy." The fourth leg started on June 28, with the Foo Fighters and Stone Temple Pilots.

By September, the band were happy that the tour was coming to an end. "I can't help but notice that this tour is ending at the right time," said Flea. "We have been working long enough… it's time to get away from it and breathe a little bit, time to get with dogs and children." John was more interested in getting the touring over with so they could get cracking with the next album: "We'll start working on

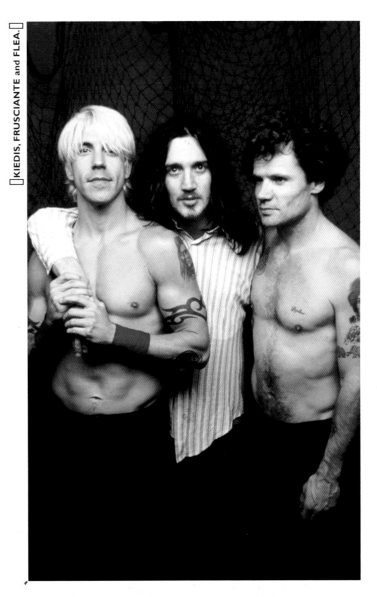

KIEDIS, FRUSCIANTE and FLEA.

our next album in November. At the moment, it's just shapes and colours in our heads, but it will be real music in a couple of months."

John had to wait a little longer before he could get his new teeth (literally – expensive dental work had repaired the damage done by his years of drug abuse) into the next Chili Peppers record. But with the success of the reunion, he could wait. All the work and the faith they placed in each other had paid dividends. *Californication* was heading towards 13 million sales.

CALiFORNiCATiON

It's a gift that's incredibly rare in bands, but it's one the Red Hot Chili Peppers have in spades – that of simply getting better and better and better. Fifteen years after the release of their debut album, four long years after the release of the darkly troubled *One Hot Minute* and with wild years, drug problems and tragic deaths thankfully behind them, the Chilis released probably the best album of their career to date. *Californication* was an amazing return to form. The Red Hot Chili Peppers won the 2000 Grammy Award for "Scar Tissue" and *Californication* also received nominations for Best Rock Album. This was now a band that could not be stopped.

Around The World

Allowing Flea to kick off the album with a monstrous bass blast was always going to be a good idea and as "Around The World" growls with renewed fury you can sense the band mentally limbering up for the fight of their lives. With "… World", they win.

"I try not to whine / but I must warn ya / 'Bout the motherfuckin" girls / From California," Anthony exclaims, sounding fresher, stronger, sharper and more focused than he has done since 1991's *Blood Sugar Sex Magik*. Flea's bass leaps from bar to bar like a steroid-fuelled gazelle; John keeps things supremely simple, with edgy garage-funk riffs and noisome explosions after each chorus;

Chad feeds in percussive flavours between his beats; but it's Anthony who stands out, his voice rich and warm, his vocals as nonsensical, and as heartfelt, as ever. On the last chorus he abandons words altogether and breaks into a string of ludicrous growls and yelps – and it still works, the band still sound on top of their game. Or as Anthony says – "Around the world / I feel dutiful / Take a wife / 'Cos life is beautiful".

Parallel Universe

As in so much of *Californication*, "Parallel Universe" is deeply in debt to John's hugely inventive, powerful guitar work. Here he sets up a wriggling, twisting riff and only loosens his grip when the song launches into its exultant chorus. Sounding angrier and yet more disciplined than ever before, Flea and Chad keep things simple, only allowing themselves to go over the edge when John's guitar takes a long, slow and phased leap into the solo. As he does, Flea takes up the twisting riff himself, allowing odd echoes of Iron Maiden's taut Eighties metal to shine through.

Anthony, after slipping almost unnoticed into a British accent at the end of the first verse ("It's getting harder and harder / To tell what came first"), assumes the mantle of "A sidewinder / I'm a California King" in the chorus as he muses on elemental questions such as the intricacies of a solar system that could fit in your eye, the stars in our minds, or how none of us really, *really* die. We have come a long way from "Catholic School Girls Rule", and no mistake.

Scar Tissue

A huge US hit, "Scar Tissue" is another of Anthony's tales of innocence lost, of drugs and separation and hurt. He is, of course, free of his own drug problems now, but just as in "Under The Bridge" – a track "Scar Tissue" resembles more than just lyrically – his elevated, solitary position of freedom from chemical dependency is a freedom that ends up feeling very similar to loneliness.

A million miles from the funked-up, skate-punk fury of so much of the band's work, this track introduces John's take on jazz and soul into the Chili Peppers mix and the result is a piece that floats above the rest of the album, weightless and driven by its own immediately memorable melody.

"Scar tissue that I wish you saw / Sarcastic Mister know-it-all", sings Anthony and he's never sounded so raw, so open. "Push me up against the wall / Young Kentucky girl in a push-up bra" or "Blood loss in a bathroom stall / Southern girl with a scarlet drawl" these are dreams and flashes from Anthony's past life, memories of a time when everything was different to the way it looks and feels now.

Otherside

Another huge US hit, this time spending in excess of 20 weeks on the Modern Rock chart and becoming a massive live favourite, "Otherside" is immensely dark fare for the ChiliPeppers.

Sounding quite unlike anything else on the record, the track is supported by Flea's rumbling bass and John's gentle guitar flurries. Anthony tells another sobriety story, this time about a departed friend who speaks to him through a photograph – the smart money's on Hillel Slovak – and how, now he knows he can never use alcohol or drugs ever again, he has to take his own personal battle on to death – to the "otherside".

One of the Chili Peppers' most adult and affecting songs, Anthony's hurt and frustration are all over the track. "I yell and tell it that / It's not my friend / I tear it down and tear it down / And then it's born again". Remarkably powerful.

Get On Top

But let's not forget who's made this album – this is still the Red Hot Chili Peppers and in tribute to their immense capacity for lurid sexuality and ridiculous,

libidinous funk, here comes "Get On Top". Immediately reminiscent of *BSSM*, lines such as "Gorilla cunt-illa / I'm an ass killer / You're ill but I'm iller" are prime Chili Peppers. Flea sounds particularly happy here, his bass playing running freely from slap-heavy funk to more punked-out fire. John's jazz persona gets a little showcase, but it's jazz in the light-fingered Hendrix sense rather than the weighty,

serious sense. The Chilis sound better here than they did a decade earlier.

Californication

One of the gentlest moments on the album, "Californication" is structured in a way that the band have never really tried before: out go the funk, the

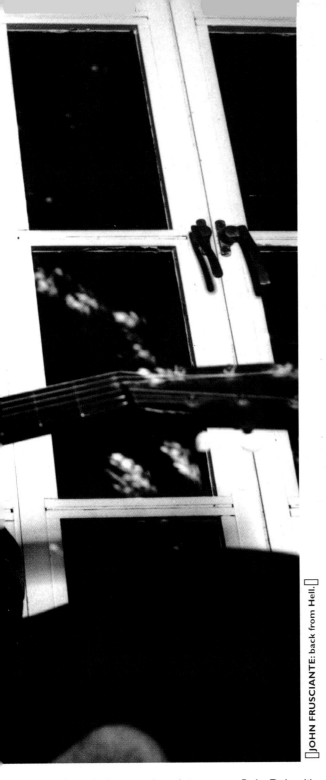

JOHN FRUSCIANTE: back from Hell.

everyone from "Psychic spies from China" to "Little girls from Sweden". The town is located on the most extreme edge of "Western civilization", which rather neatly means it's the setting sun's final location every day of every week of every year.

Anthony sounds at once both horrified ("Celebrity skin is this your chin") and amused ("Space may be the final frontier / But it's made in a Hollywood basement") by California and its impact on the world around him, But while he rails against a "teenage bride with a baby inside / who gets high off information" and wonders if his dead friend Kurt Cobain can hear "The spheres / Singing songs off Station To Station", he knows that California is, thanks to its unique geological faults, locked in a cycle of renewal and rebirth – and if there's one thing Keidis likes, it's rebirth. "Destruction is a very rough road / But it also breeds creation / And earthquakes are to a girl's guitar / They're just another good vibration".

Ultimately, he can't resist Californication anymore than the rest of the world can.

Easily

One of the crucial tracks that makes *Californication* the album it is, "Easily" is a showcase for one of Anthony's most oblique lyrics as well as one of John Frusciante's most beautiful guitar solos. The band and producer Rick Rubin have cooked up a garage-band sound reminiscent of their early demos, but there's all the weight and depth here that those tracks could never achieve.

Anthony's lyrics touch on the futility of war, the teachings of Shao Lin, the empty uselessness of celebrity. And in a heartwarming move after stories of loneliness and remorse, such as "Scar Tissue", Anthony's growing love and commitment to his girlfriend Yohanna – who insisted in a *Rolling Stone* interview that Anthony's most rock-star characteristic was his amazingly shiny teeth – was

punk and the metal and in come Bob Dylan-like analogy, namechecking, the ascending and descending chord patterns of The Beatles and, at its heart, the endless round of love/hate/love/hate battles that Anthony has with his adopted state.

Hollywood and the lies and fantasies it peddles makes up much of the theme behind "Californication"; its silver-screen dreams draw in

beginning to emerge in a few tracks on the album.

"Easily let's get carried away / Easily let's get married today" he sings, clearly aware of how brief and painful life can be. "Calling calling for something in the air / Calling calling I know you must be there".

Porcelain

The closest the Chili Peppers will ever come to sounding like a soul band, "Porcelain" is drenched in a soporific jazz flavour; much of the track appears to be wrapped in cotton wool, which, bearing in mind the opiate-esque flow of the lyrics, is most appropriate. Another track that's not so much anti-heroin as pointing out the hopelessness of its regular use, lyrics such as "Are you wasting away in your skin?" and "Can you bear not to share with your child" suggest someone in a progressed pregnant state who is still using. "Drifting and floating and fading away," Anthony sings. "Nodding and melting and fading away". There's no redemption at the end, no sense of change or hope. A bleak, bleak track.

protracted gold-tooth phase. Is Emit Remmus about Sporty Spice, Mel C was asked by fans on her website. "I don't know you'd have to ask Anthony Kiedis," she replied, rather noncommittally. "It would be nice if it was though, wouldn't it!"

Kiedis himself said, "I started writing the lyrics for 'Emit Remmus' before I ever met Sporty, but I finished them after I'd known her for a bit, so you figure it out…"

Whatever the truth is, the track itself is a fiery burst of noise with a huge, bass-heavy chorus from Flea and one of John's finest solos.

I Like Dirt

One of Anthony's finest "Hello trees! Hello sky!" moments, "I Like Dirt" has the same back-to-nature sentiments as "The Righteous & The Wicked" from *BSSM* and "Green Heaven" from *RHCP* but the simple message of the power of Mother Earth is tied up with an overtly sexual message in the lyrics.

"The earth is made of dirt and wood / And I'd be water if I could," Anthony sings, the lyrics touched with a strong rap inflection as Flea rolls out one of his most boogie-heavy bass lines and John peels off a series of stabbing guitar runs.

"Some come up and some come young / Live to love and give good tongue" – now that does sound familiar, doesn't it?

Emit Remmus

Perfect – on an album named in tribute to the debilitating effects of American popular culture, a track that names more London sights than The Kinks' "Waterloo Sunset" as it tells the tale of Anthony's brief liaison with former Sporty Spice, Mel C. Sound unlikely? Well, that's what everyone else thought, but the evidence is there, in main from the two people themselves.

"The California flower is a poppy child," Anthony sings, referring to himself. But who's the "Felony" who sends him "all the gold" in her smile? Could the felony be Melanie (C)? After all, Sporty Spice certainly had a

This Velvet Glove

Another one of *Californication*'s love songs, "This Velvet Glove" is for Kiedis' girlfriend Yohanna ("Your solar eyes are like / Nothing I have ever seen / Somebody close / That I can see right through"), a reflection on his time spent in addictive behaviour ("It's such a waste to be wasted / In the first place") and a tribute to the grace of John, who rejoined the band to record this album after nearly killing himself with heroin ("John says to live above hell / My will is well"). Though the line does sound like one ex-user talking to another, Kiedis told *Juice* magazine that, yes,

the John was John Frusciante, but added that he was not quoting him literally – the lyric was lifted from one of John's solo works.

"He was singing about living life above hell," Anthony said, "meaning whether from drugs or just state of mind. He'd sampled life living in hell, he thought better of it, got over it and was living in a more beautiful space. I was so deeply in love when I wrote it, and John was very much a part of my life during that time, creating good energy so I wanted to mention it."

SaVior

Never before have the Chili Peppers sounded much like that other great but troubled Californian outfit The Beach Boys, but during "Savior"'s floatingly psychedelic chorus, Kiedis and company come close for the first time.

One of the more ponderous tracks on *Californication*, "Savior" has a truly wonderful Kiedis vocal, his voice a huge, rich beast utterly unlike the thin growl he experimented with for so long, but the time signatures shift uneasily and the is-he-or-isn't-he references to a God-like character make the track more than a little unwieldy. However, this being the Chili Peppers, the song couldn't be left totally alone in its po-faced religiosity, not when there are lyrics such as, "We are the Red Hots / And we're loving up the love me nots / The flowers in your flower pots / Are dancing on the table tops" on offer. What this has to do with Jesus and friends, no one knows.

Purple StAin

While Anthony might not sound anything like he used to, while Rick Rubin's production might be ten times what anyone else managed, while John Frusciante might be clean and serene, some things in the Chili camp never change. And one of those things is the traditional blatantly sexual track near the end of an album. "Party On Your Pussy", "Sexy Mexican Maid", "Sir Psycho Sexy" – the list, if not endless, is certainly fairly comprehensive. To this canon we must add "Purple Stain",

Californication's only real throwback to the Chilis of old.

Almost – because "Purple Stain" just doesn't really cut it. While "To finger paint is not a sin / I put my middle finger in / Your monthly blood is what I win" is suitably graphic, and "Python power straight from Monty / Celluloid loves got a John Frusciante" is a neat line, the rest of the track seems to fall a little flat. Powerful production aside, "Purple Stain" could have come from *Freaky Styley* and backwards moves are never to be encouraged…

Right On Time

… except when they're this cool. "Right On Time" is pure disco-punk-funk, never slacking off for a single second, Flea's bass barely able to keep up with the breakneck pace of the track. Though "Right…" is already nearly five years old, it wouldn't sound out of place in many a DJ's electroclash set, so potent is its noisy, beat-driven fervour. Don't go looking for insight in the lyrics, though. "Holy cow bow wow wow / Now I'm here I'm nowhere now" is one of the more profound on offer.

Road Trippin'

A wonderfully chilled end to the record, "Road Trippin'", featuring Patrick Warren on the swirling, circling Chamberlin organ, closes *Californication* on a sombre but uplifting note. A deeply romantic and simple tale of a road trip during which three friends escape the city and find a new and more enlightening life while busy getting lost on the byways of the USA, it's a farewell to the madness of fame and addiction. "These smiling eyes are just a mirror for the sun," Anthony sings; the endless California sunset, the one alluded to in the title track, is clearly audible in his voice. "Now let us check our heads / And let us check the surf / Staying high and dry's / More trouble than it's worth / In the sun".

The Chilis had returned triumphantly with *Californication*, but could they keep up the momentum? It would be three years before we got to find out.

8 'By The Way'

By December, 2000, stories were emerging from the Chili Peppers' camp that work on the follow-up to *Californication* was due to start early in 2001. When picking up a couple of gongs at the MY VH1 awards ceremony, Flea told Reuters that the band would be going into a studio the following February and that, although the decision as to who was going to produce the record had not been made, Rick Rubin would certainly be involved. "He's actually been like an angel in my life. I love him," said Flea. He claimed that they had no great masterplan for the recording of the album, rather that they would be going for spontaneity in the studio. "That's when the magic happens," he said. Flea also revealed that he had recently been working with former Chili Peppers drummer Cliff Martinez and Herbie Hancock on the soundtrack for the Steven Soderbergh movie *Traffic*.

In January 2001, Rubin was officially confirmed as producer for the next Chili Peppers album. "He makes subtle, little, well-focused, well-thought-out changes in the arrangement in songs and basically lays there and lets you do your thing," said Kiedis. Meanwhile, January saw the band appear at the enormous Rock In Rio festival, Brazil, before which the band jammed some ideas around. "We rehearsed for a few days before the South America shows," John Frusciante told dotmusic.com while in Europe promoting his third solo album, *To Record Only Water For Ten Days*. "We were jamming and coming up with ideas for new songs. It was great and I love the new sound so much."

He went to say that the jam sessions had reminded him of early Public Image Limited, a sign that the band was exploring its musical influences as part of the recording process. Flea had been playing with a pick and was learning Peter Hook's Joy Division bass lines. "There are a lot of new rhythms and sounds for people to hear. Everything we do, it's going to be fresh," Frusciante confirmed.

The band were working on the album for real in February, and reports emerging from the sessions were encouraging. "Whatever the energy on *Californication* is, it's that energy multiplied," said Frusciante on the progression of the recording. In April 2001, Flea announced that he wouldn't be involved in the Jane's Addiction reunion tour that was due to kick off on April because he wanted to spend more time working on the Chilis' album.

The rest of 2001 was spent writing, recording and playing shows. And, although the year was dotted with occasional Chili Peppers news, it was clear that the band had their heads down and were working hard to come up with an album that would be a worthy successor to *Californication*.

They spent part of the recording process in the Chateau Marmont, the vintage chic rock star hotel on LA's Sunset Strip where Anthony had been living. In room 78 on the seventh floor, at the back of the building furthest away from the traffic noise, the band

set up a computer recording system in one room, **with the** microphone in the other, and went about the process of creating *By The Way*. Anthony was asked by *Rolling Stone* whether they'd had any complaints from any of the other guests at the hotel. "Not really," he replied, "because the majority of it is in headphones. The loudest thing you can hear is me singing and screaming. The only comment I got was when I got in an elevator with this absolutely adorable and sexy girl from somewhere in the British Isles: 'What is going on in that room? Someone is singing real loud.' And I said, 'Well, that was me, making a record.' She's like, 'Oh, OK. I was enjoying it, actually. Even when it was antagonising me, I was enjoying it, because I'm a novelist and I'm in there writing next door to you. What you were doing kind of inspired me to get my writing going.' Unfortunately, that was the only encounter I ever had with her."

John Frusciante threw more light on the album's creation, talking to *Guitar* magazine: "I wanted this album to have more dimension, more different sounds and more movements in the chord progressions. But I also wanted it to be more fun." He also revealed how he had been getting interested in vocal harmonies, one of the most notable developments of the band's songwriting skills and sound, and had wanted to incorporate what he was learning into the new record: "Me and Rick Rubin would get together every day, and he's got these CDs of AM radio hits from the Sixties. And they'd have stuff by the Mamas and Papas and songs like 'Cherish' by The Association and 'Georgy Girl' by The Seekers. Those songs are all about harmonies."

Anthony also talked about the influences that had been in the air while making the album: "The Beatles are clearly an influence, and doo-wop, as well as some other stuff coming out the 1950s." The recordings went so well that it felt to the band as if they couldn't stop writing songs. They had 40 pieces of music and had to choose just 28 to work on; of those, 16 made it onto the finished album.

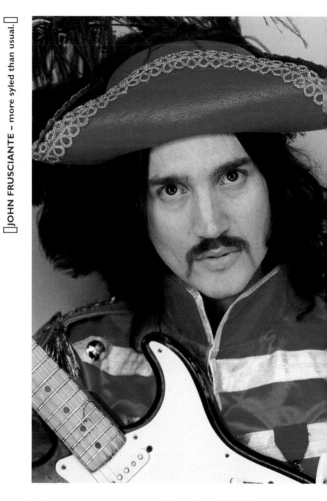

JOHN FRUSCIANTE – more syled than usual.

In June it was announced that the Chili Peppers would be awarded the Buddy Award by the Musician's Assistance Program (MAP) for their support of the organization, which provides addiction treatment for musicians. MAP was the organization that had helped Frusciante quit his own addictions.

In August, world events caught up with the band. They were forced to cancel a show in Israel. More than 20,000 tickets had been sold for the gig in Tel Aviv, but two suicide bombings earlier in the month had convinced the band that they should postpone the show, despite former president Bill Clinton urging them to play. They did, however, play the V2001 festival in the UK and supported U2 at Slane Castle.

A mark of the Chili Peppers' standing in the world came in October when Elton John announced

that he had hoped to have Chad, Flea and John record as his backing band for his album, *Songs From The West Coast*. "Flea is my favourite bass player of all time," said the diminutive piano player. "The thing with the Chili Peppers I was interested in is that they leave gaps, and their songs are very open." He might also have been quite interested in the fact that they had racked up 13 million sales for *Californication*.

With no sign of the album throughout 2001, people were clamouring for Chili Pepper news in 2002. John Frusciante gave little away when he told the press that "we have a completely new sound. We've given a lot of thought to music in the past year and half and we've gotten really tight." A June release date was revealed, along with some festival dates, and it was also announced that the band were to play a

show on July 9, now also the release date of the album, *By The Way*, "in the shadow of the Statue Of Liberty" on Ellis Island, in recognition of the regeneration of downtown New York following the terrorist attacks of September 11, 2001.

The Red Hot Chili Peppers finally unleashed their eighth album, *By The Way*, three years after the release of *Californication*. It entered the UK album chart at the top spot, and the day the album was released in the US, the single, also called "By The Way", was already at number one in the US *Billboard* Modern Rock chart, helped along by a video clip that featured Anthony being kidnapped by a mullet-wearing taxi driver who happens to be a fan. Somehow, the track manages to deliver the punky funk thrash that still lies at the root of the Chili Peppers' sound, yet also builds on the slightly more pensive and almost pop-oriented feel that they had developed. John Frusciante tried to sum it up: "It's very different from our last record, but the soul of it, the foundation of it, the four of us playing, is still the same. But there's a lot going on and there's a lot of sounds coming from all over the place and a lot of different styles being combined and a lot of vocal harmonies."

The album was another massive success, with some extraordinary critical reversals taking place in some sections of the media. One American reviewer went as far as to say the album "proved" that the Red Hot Chili Peppers were a better studio band than their "outrageous live reputation would lead you to believe" and reckoned that *By The Way* was a Red Hot Chili Peppers album "even a mother could love – the one that could win them the top Grammy". John Robinson in *NME* wrote that "their hearts are on their sleeves, for sure, but their hearts seem to be in their work as well." The *Independent* said that the band were now "firmly into Grammy-winning maturity" while *The Times* noted that the band's huge success had made them more stable than ever and praised their new-found "fine sense of melody". And later in the year, they were dubbed "The Best In The World" at the annual *Kerrang!* awards. Within a month or so of release, *By The Way* had sold more than three million copies and was certified multi-platinum in the USA and the UK.

At the end of 2002, EMI announced the March 2003 re-release of the Chili Peppers' first four albums, all remastered and featuring bonus tracks, and huge shows were scheduled all over the world. The single "Can't Stop" was released in February 2003 and in March the band arrived in the UK for six sold-out shows at Glasgow SECC, London Docklands and the Manchester Evening News Arena. While the band were in the country, tickets went on sale for the their concert at Ireland's Slane Castle in August. They'd last played there in 2001 with U2 headlining, and they were returning, this time as triumphant headliners. On March 7, all 80,000 tickets sold in two-and-a-half hours. It was the second-fastest-selling show in Irish music history, beaten only by the U2 show two years previously.

The remainder of the year saw the Chili Peppers gigging and recording, and the release of a greatest hits collection (called, prosaically enough, *Greatest Hits And Videos*), this time one that actually had some hits on it, unlike their previous EMI collection, which they had insisted was called *What Hits!?*.

Two new songs, "Fortune Faded" and "History", were recorded for the greatest hits collection, which was released in November, as was the DVD of the band's monumental show at Slane Castle.

"Fortune Faded", released as a single in November 2003, gives an indication as to the direction of the next album, and Flea offers some more insights on the band's official website: "We wrote and recorded 15 songs and they rock. We played a wide variety of music arranged into song format that is among the most diverse and dynamic, good-feeling shit we have ever done, at least that's how it feels to me. We gave it no thought. We just rocked and it worked well, it is the fastest we have ever recorded so much material." Alternatively, you might prefer to believe Flea when he told nme.com that the new songs "sound like Bulgarian pygmies if you crossed them with Transylvanian choir groups".

What's next for the Red Hot Chili Peppers? The next album is going to have to be a corker of almost supernatural quality if they're going to better the success of their previous two efforts. Maybe they've come as far as they can. Certainly, Anthony has felt it's now time for his autobiography, suggesting perhaps that he feels the story has reached some level of completion. Due out late in 2004, it's being co-written with Larry Sloman, who also worked with the radio DJ Howard Stern on his book *Private Parts*. But it's John Frusciante's immense talent that is energizing the band now. You have the feeling that he is just coming into his prime as an artist, and that the Red Hot Chili Peppers will remain the perfect home for his considerable abilities for some time to come.

The Red Hot Chili Peppers are now one of the most successful and sophisticated rock groups in the world, and their story is one of epic struggle, redemption and finally massive success, both creatively and commercially. But we will never forget that they were once that band who wore socks on their cocks. And, to their eternal credit, neither will they.

By The Way

"I always felt we had a real femininity to our music," Flea told *Guitar World* magazine prior to the release of *By The Way*. "But it's not heard so much when something is really loud, distorted and *jammy*. To me the biggest difference on *By The Way* is that there are more *songs*."

By The Way

Eighteen years after the release of their scratchy debut and three years after the glorious return of *Californication*, the Red Hot Chili Peppers returned with an old guitarist – John Frusciante, back after a six-year heroin holiday – and a totally fresh take on their sound. Where once they battered listeners with macho power, they now cruised and glided on wheels oiled by a new obsession: harmony and melody were the Chili Peppers' new gods. The band's first single, "By The Way", was full of deliriously melting harmonies, with Anthony and Flea's voices in perfect accord.

"The song is about the color of any given night in Los Angeles," Anthony told *Spin* magazine. "What's going on in the streets, from a crime in a parking garage to a sexy little girl named Annie singing songs to some guy who she's got a crush on. It's an atmospheric lyric – just painting a picture rather than a whole plot. The feeling is one of waiting, hoping and wanting to make a connection with another person. A romantic connection. That feeling of, 'Is this gonna be the night?'!"

It was a theme that he would revisit elsewhere on the record.

Universally Speaking

The mid-ground between New Order' s "Vanishing Point" and The Supremes' "Where Did Our Love Go?" is not a well-worn path, but after hearing "Universally Speaking" you'll wonder why, because this mix of sounds and styles produced one of the album's highlights. While apparently fitting well into Kiedis' list of "Love songs – in a very obscure, less than obvious way", the track also celebrates the release and pleasure that a freedom from sustained, regular drug use can bring. "I saw your crime / Dying to get high / Two of a kind / Beats all hands tonight" Anthony sings as Flea peals out a bass-solo New Order's Peter Hook would be proud of. "While we were making the new album I was listening to the new wave British synth-pop, Human League's two first albums, *Reproductions* and *Travelogue*," John told *Guitar World*. "They are weird, entirely electronic pop records. I also listened to glitter rock, Mott The Hoople and Gary Glitter, funny music, because I wanted *By The Way* to be a happy-spirited album." And it is, and this is a great, under-celebrated Chilis track.

This Is The Place

A deeply layered piece in which Anthony confronts the nature of addiction itself and finds the root of his problems buried in his own DNA strands, the building blocks of his own life that he inherited from his parents. "I don't want to do it / Like my daddy did / I don't want to give it / To my baby's kid," Anthony sings as John's guitar hangs like the ghost of a dream in the air around his head. The melodies and harmonies that "By The Way" introduced get another huge outing, this time in a defiantly Eighties tone that somehow – oddly, perhaps – doesn't recall the band's own Eighties works.

Dosed

More of Anthony's love songs to someone he hasn't met yet, "Dosed" is a little unspectacular, but the chorus has a keening, almost country yearn in it, which is another very new departure for the band. Talking to *Spin* magazine, Anthony commented, "The songs on this album are either about being in love or the desire to be in love. It's definitely what I've been feeling for the last year. A profound sense of wanting love in my daily experience," and "Dosed" is full of that longing. "In you a star is born / You cut a perfect form / Someone forever warm," he sings, his voice thick with hopes and regrets.

Don't Forget Me

From the DNA of addiction to the voice that guides the addicted to a more peaceful, safe place, "Don't

Forget Me" sees Anthony present himself as both the drug and the energy that can be the addict's saviour. "I'm an ocean in your bedroom / Make you feel warm / Make you want to reassume," he sings – a reference to reassuming the position, i.e., the foetal position. "I'm the rainbow in your jail cell / All the memories of / Everything you've ever smelled /Not alone I'll be there."

"Don't Forget Me" touches on the mystical love that Kiedis insists kept him safe through his own years of addiction. "It's about that spirit of universal love and the spirit of God," he told *Spin* magazine. "Whatever that might be to you. I don't mean it in a religious sense at all. Let's just call it an energy, or beauty. That energy is everywhere. It doesn't turn its back on people because they're fuckups, losers and dope fiends. For me, that beauty has always been there, even when I was dying. It's infinite. It's in the jail cells. It's in the ocean. It's in all of us. It's there when you're born and it's waiting for you when you die."

The Zephyr Song

At one stage this was called "Coltrane", so marked was its cap-doffing to sax-playing jazz legend John, a huge hero to both Flea and that other John, Frusciante – but that doesn't mean the non-jazz fan should live in fear. A truly uplifting moment after the dark waters sailed by "Dosed" and "Don't Forget Me", "The Zephyr Song" is one of the easiest, most unaffected tracks on the album. There's no dark subtext to "Zephyr", no aching need to be understood, just the sound of a band in love with all the possibilities music has to offer – John's ringing, early-Sixties-influenced guitar solo, the phased simplicity of the backing vocals and Anthony's impassioned offer to "Fly away on my Zephyr / We'll find a place together".

And speaking of Zephyrs, in 2002 the documentary *Dogtown and Z-Boys* followed the formation of one of skateboarding's most famous images of the Seventies: the pool-riding Zephyr surf team (Z-Boys), drawn from the most hardcore locals-only crews in California's Santa Monica beach slums. Another direct influence on the song.

Can't Stop

At the end of the band's previous tour, John had settled back at home by studying musical theory. He would sit and listen to The Beatles, the supremely talented jazz bassist Charles Mingus and the songs of Burt Bacharach and Hal David and despite "Can't Stop" being the closest to a "Give It Away"-style chest-beater that *BTW* gets, John cannot hide the musical invention rippling underneath his own fractured, jagged funk riff. From the circular jazz figure of the intro through the Beatles harmonies in the backing vocals to the off-beat handclaps inspired by avant-garde composers such as Philip Glass, "Can't Stop" is a serious leap on from anything the Chilis had done before, but was also melodic and desirable enough to provide them with one of their biggest radio hits for years.

Lyrically Anthony revisits some of his favourite themes – Native American reservations, rock-funk pioneers Defunkt, the Sex Pistols, drugs ("Can I get two maybe three of these") and, naturally, sex: "I'll get you into penetration / The gender of a generation". He even finds time to throw in his odd English accent, first heard on "Police Helicopter" on the band's debut album.

"Invention leads to making music with a wider variety of emotion," John told *Spin* magazine. "It makes me see even more how infinite music is."

I Could Die For You

Another heart-emptying plea for love that's structured like an old Barry White or Curtis Mayfield hit, a string of hooks that end up making the song sound utterly anthemic, without sounding like either of those inspirational figures. The track focuses on the perfection of just one partner and the love and devotion that Anthony could give to them. In his eyes the love would never be sullied,

and the purity of his love makes the song sound like a hymn to an unborn child, the words a father would offer to his own son or daughter – "I'm here to be your only go-between / To tell you of the sights eyes have seen". Unlike so many of his other songs, there's no hint of sensuality, just devotion and hope. "I could die for you / Whatchu want to do / On this life I choose".

Midnight

Flea's love of classical music is right to the fore here with a brooding string quartet intro leading into a whirling ballad touched by trip-hoppy, dustbowl atmospherics reminiscent of early Portishead, a beautifully understated guitar line from John and some darkly oblique lyrics from Anthony that touch on jazz ("Resonating in the shape of things to come" – George Benson's album , *The Shape Of Things To Come* was released in 1968), underground film-maker Kenneth Anger

("The blood of Scorpio's a nine / The rising moon is on the shine" – Anger's masterpiece, *Scorpio Rising* was released in 1964), even Buddhism ("We are the lotus kids / Better take note of this" – The Lotus Kids is a dance performed on Vesak Day, an important Buddhist festival, commemorating the birth, enlightenment and death of the Buddha).

Tracks such as "Midnight", in which – again – John's backing vocals lift the track effortlessly above the norm, show the Chilis growing in ways that would have seem unimaginable in their early days. As Chad noted, "With bands that have been

around for 20 or 25 years, you get a kind of musical telepathy. You can't manufacture that, it can only happen from just doing it, being connected and wanting to be connected."

Throw Away Your Television

If "Midnight" was an amazing vision of the future, then "Throw Away Your Television" is like an unwelcome trawl through the past. Somehow managing to dredge up memories of "True Men Don't Kill Coyotes" from their debut album, "… Television" is the one weak spot on an otherwise exemplary album. Flea attempts to funk things up, but Chad's rolling, tribal drums, John's thin guitar lines and Anthony's overly simplistic lyrics – "Throw away your television / Take the noose from your ambition now" – just sound tired. "It's a repeat of a story told / It's a repeat and it's getting old". Indeed.

CabrOn

A South American-flavoured love song written from the point of view of a young Mexican man who's

JOHN FRUSCIANTE in Grandma's sweater.

developing a taste for love ("I will get it on with you"), or for tequila ("I am small but I am strong"). The Spanish word "Cabron" in Mexico can mean either "bastard" or "boss", but either way it is a word with strong connotations. When a drinks company called Tecabroniza tried to launch a brew called "Tequila Cabron" in 1999, they were told it was unacceptable; officials at the Mexican Federal Consumer Protection Agency ruled the name profane and fined the company $27,500.

It was an unusual piece for the Chili Peppers, who usually work as a unit on songs with pieces of music constructed then given to Anthony so that he can decide which ones he wants to sing on. "Cabron" was different. This time, John worked alongside Anthony in developing the song, as the singer told *Spin* magazine: "John and I got together in his room at the Chateau Marmont, where he was living at the time. 'Cabron' sounded like he'd written it to be a flamenco guitar instrumental. I just loved it, but it took Chad and Flea a while to find their places in it because it was so different and weird for us, coming from left field."

Left field indeed, "Cabron" finds John on acoustic guitar and utilizing a capo. This device, which clamps on to the fretboard and raises the pitch of the strings, was much loved by two of his heroes – ex-Smiths guitarist Johnny Marr and British prog-rock legends, Jethro Tull, whose album, *Aqualung* John listened to a lot before writing the song. In another musical move unusual for the Chilis, Flea plays an acoustic bass.

Tear

Reminiscent of "Under The Bridge" in many ways – the band even consciously mimic the guitar part that leads into that song's chorus in the bridge – "Tear" is *By The Way*'s most downbeat moment. Anthony's cry from the heart comes coloured with literary and drug allusions ("Coming on strong / Baudelaire / Seems to me like / All the world gets high") before a massed harmony chorus erupts that recalls the early Seventies West Coast folk rock of Crosby, Stills, Nash & Young or The Eagles. This is certainly a long way from "Good Time Boys", and another sign of the dramatic growth and vision the band enjoyed during the making of the album.

On Mercury

A huge favourite live, "On Mercury" is a curious blend of rough-hewn, Sixties Jamaican ska and Fifties American pop and a chance for Anthony to not only try out a few odd accents – check the first verse in particular – but also to drag up childhood recollections, namecheck early rock and roll tunes and mention babies again. How broody can one man get over the course of one record? Very, it would seem – Anthony would later split with girlfriend Yohanna Logan when it became apparent that his desire to have children was not reciprocated. The lyric, "Looking up into a reverse vertigo", describes the sensation of staring hard at the stars and feeling the immenseness of space pulling you up into the darkness, while "Sit up straight / I'm on a double date" refers his habit of double-dating at LA restaurants with his father, the actor Blackie Dammett, during the latter's visits. Flea drives the track, his bass providing the melodic backbone for the song, while John's guitar subsumes itself in support to the massed choirs of sighing backing vocals. Nevertheless, the overall feel is of Anthony's space-age flights of fancy.

Minor Thing

John's love of Eighties British heroes The Smiths shines through again on this track. His fluid, jangling guitar recalls Johnny Marr's playing on tracks such as "Cemetery Gates" or "Big Mouth Strikes Again", but the track soon breaks out into a melodic funk track with Anthony providing a short and rather unexpected rap. But this Chili Peppers rap is of the 2002 variety, a hugely different beast from their old, more full-on way of doing things. As Chad Smith told

Rolling Stone "There's a lot of stuff that I hear on the radio or on TV or at halftime of a sporting event and it's like, Jesus Christ – the kids today are really getting short-changed! I hope they can get turned on to something cooler than that. But rather than trashing that which sucks and is lame, I'd rather create something beautiful."

The band have certainly succeeded here. After the second chorus John's guitar erupts over the track, but it's the briefest of intrusions, a flash of colour before a key change turns "Minor Thing" into a booming, cinematic epic.

Warm Tape

"Warm" is word that turns up again and again in the Chili Peppers – it's already appeared twice on *BTW* in "Dosed" and "Don't Forget Me". It's most at home on "Warm Tape" though, another song with a space-age, horror-movie tinge, in which Anthony manages to sound like Blur's Damon Albarn on the British band's classic "The Universal". "Warm Tape' is another one of Anthony's yearning love songs, carried by sweeping synths, Flea's gently grooving bass lines and Chad's rolling, jazz-tinged drums. On recent tours Anthony has introduced the song by saying, "If you're thinking about having sex and making babies, do it to this song", which seems appropriate when you look at the lyrics because, while most of this album was recorded post-break-up with Anthony's long-time girlfriend Yohanna, the raw sensuality never gets frozen out by the pain and the loss. "I know I make it for two / Intuition's only what you take from it / I know I make it for two / You were there and I was fortunate".

Venice Queen

An album with the scope of *By The Way* needs a finale to be proud of and "Venice Queen" is certainly that. The song is a tribute to Gloria Scott, a Los Angeles drug counsellor who died of cancer shortly after the band appeared at a benefit concert for her alongside Neil Young. Scott, who had battled her own years of addiction before cleaning up and helping many musicians and others addicted to alcohol and drugs, was a great friend of Anthony's and a source of much inspiration and peace. "I'm good at losing," Anthony muttered to *Spin* magazine. "It's one of my specialties."

The song itself is surely one of his most open declarations of love to someone who changed – if not outright saved – his life. As the music swells behind him, John's acoustic guitar and soaring vocals spinning on with a momentum of their own, Anthony sings, "And now it's time for you to go / You taught me most of what I know / Where would I be without you Glo / G. L. O R. I. A. / Is love my friend". His words fade out and only John's guitar remains. Scott was an integral part of the team that aided the guitarist in his battle with drug addiction. Had she not been around, then, who knows, perhaps this band – who, over 20 years, have produced some of the most powerful music of their time – wouldn't exist either.

FRUSCIANTE: he just stepped out of a salon, you know.

131

9 John Frusciante Solo Albums

The first public appearance of John Frusciante's solo work came on the Jane's Addiction video, *The Gift*, with the track "Ants", which was later available on the cassette version of his debut solo album.

John's first solo album was the result of recordings he'd been doing throughout his tenure in The Red Hot Chili Peppers, recording bits and pieces on a small four-track machine in hotel rooms while on tour, and more work he'd done since leaving the band on a small machine in his home. Considering that he was being plagued by voices telling him what to do, and was feeling a considerable amount of anguish about his impending decision to quit the band – and also that, after quitting the band, he plunged headlong into large-scale drug indulgence – it's no surprise that this collection makes for difficult listening. It's lo-fi, experimental and dense; some would call it self-indulgent. John claimed that he'd wanted to release it under a fake name, that of a fictional 1960s character, and that the second half of the album was "written for string quartet".

Featuring two tracks with River Phoenix playing guitar and singing ("We had a communication that was intense," said John of recording with River), the album was the result of John's prodigious output rate at the time. He claimed to have written 70 songs after releasing this collection of 25. There seemed to be an almost wilful effort on his part to emulate the downfall of 1960s pop burnout Syd Barrett. Barrett left Pink Floyd in the late 1960s. Partly thanks to his huge appetite for LSD, Barrett was in a bad state when he quitted the band. He recorded two solo albums of Syd weirdness and then disappeared from the music scene, rumoured to be holed up either at his mother's house or in an institution. Frusciante was definitely in the process of severing his already tenuous links to reality when he recorded *Niandra Landes…*.

"I was thinking about him [Syd Barrett] a lot at that time," Frusciante confirmed. According to American Recordings' retail marketing man, Danny Ornela, the reaction "Oh my God, this is insane…" was not uncommon when the album was played to record store managers. John dedicated the record to Flea's daughter, Clara, whom he described as "the strongest person I have ever met".

Reviewers (those who bothered) were left floundering by the album's oblique experimentalism. Those in favour took refuge in abstract, emotional reactions to the music: "It's scary because the roads are so unfamiliar and illogical. But it's also warm, like a caress, there's a haunting, evocative touch within its broad spaces." Most other folk decided it was the just the kind of mad gibberish you'd expect from a young rock star with a drug problem and too much time and money on his hands.

"If they have any imagination, if their heads are capable of tripping out, they'll get it," Frusciante said when asked what Chili Peppers fans might make of it.

Unlike its creator, the album didn't enjoy a critical resurrection when it was re-released in 2003: "Doesn't sound any better one decade later," said *Rolling Stone*.

Frusciante's second album was, if anything, even less approachable than the first. Rumours were rife that he'd let the tapes for this album go because he needed money after having allowed heroin and cocaine addiction to reduce him to poverty. It may explain why he later withdrew the album. Apparently he "didn't feel comfortable" with it being available for people to buy and listen to.

Even fans of Frusciante (and they were thin on the ground during these "lost" years) concede that he

sounds as if he was high when he recorded many of the songs. The inclusion of juvenilia such as "A Fall Thru The Ground" (recorded when he was 17) did nothing to improve his standing with the world's music critics. At least, one fan noted, each song on this album had its very own title, an improvement on the untitled mess of tunes on his previous effort. A generous consensus is that this was an album of some good guitar playing wrecked by dreadful singing, with the majority of listeners left bewildered and agreeing with John's later conclusion that by this point in his life, he was thought of as "finished".

Some still claim that this album, and its predecessor, will one day be hailed as works of genius. They might be the work of a genius, but this particular genius was whacked off his skull with the most mind-numbing, creativity-draining drugs available when he recorded them. Despite the best efforts of devoted fans who understandably admire John Frusciante and his artistic impulse, it might just be that he was right to remove this album from circulation.

Frusciante's third album was a shock for listeners who had become accustomed to the rambling, incoherent fruits of his solo recordings. *To Record Only Water For Ten Days* was a far more straightforward effort with recognizable song structures and was received relatively warmly, although it was still clearly a lo-fi, demo-like recording, particularly when compared to the work he was now producing with the Chili Peppers.

Apparently still dealing with the years of drug addiction, perhaps the album will be seen as the third of some kind of heroin trilogy – from the first ravages and enlightenments of a heavily opiated mind, through to the nadir of poverty and ill health that is represented by the choices which led to the release of *Smile From The Street You Hold*, and ending with the fragile recuperation of *To Record Only Water For Ten Days*.

The album's mood is predominately melancholy, with a couple of instrumentals that do little to lift the mood. John's voice, often a source of derision previously, is sounding better, but it's still a fairly

eccentric sound for most casual listeners, straying as it does into emotional falsetto quite regularly. It is, of course, a technique he has employed on recent Chili Peppers records with much more success. It's interesting to hear him testing out new ideas and approaches that later emerge in Chili Pepper recordings, and in some ways perhaps these solo albums serve as a series of sketchbooks in which the future of the Red Hot Chili Peppers can be discerned. But only if you listen really, *really* hard.

2001 INTERNET ALBUM/FROM THE SOUNDS INSIDE

2001

1 So Would Have I

2 Three Thoughts

3 I Go Through These Wall

4 Murmur

5 Saturation (Un-mastered version)

6 Interstate Sex

7 Dying (I Don't Mind)

8 The Battle of Time

9 With Love

10 I Will Always Be Beat Down

11 Fallout (Un-mastered version)

12 Penetrate Time (Lou Bergs)

13 Slow Down

14 Nature Falls

15 Beginning Again

16 Cut Myself Out

17 Place To Drive

18 How High

19 Fallout (Alternative version)

20 Leaving You

21 Sailing Outdoors

In a laudable move, the refreshed and drug-free John Frusciante gave away 21 songs to his fans via the internet. Still pretty lo-fidelity, the recordings were more coherent than his previous solo offerings. The "album" has two names because it was initially made available without a name, and was widely referred to as the *2001 Internet Album*. Following two rounds of voting on the John Frusciante website, a new name was decided upon: *From The Sounds Inside*. Perhaps this set of John's solo wanderings will be seen as the preview to the new album which, at the time of writing, is yet to be released. *From The Sounds Inside* is available for free download at http://www.johnfrusciante.com/main.html

SHADOWS COLLIDE WITH PEOPLE

Feb 2004

According to John, this is "the best music I've ever done". It was finished before the first leg of the Chili Peppers' European tour and features Chad Smith on drums and Flea on bass for two tracks. Given that this is a solo album from the man who has not only come back from the dead himself, but also re-energized the Red Hot Chili Peppers and made them the most successful rock band in the world, anticipation around this release is high. But then again, we know that John likes to explore different dimensions on his solo albums…

NIANDRA LADES AND USUALLY JUST A T-SHIRT

American Recordings November 1994

1 As Can Be

2 My Smile Is A Rifle

3 Head (Beach Arab)

4 Big Takeover

5 Curtains

6 Running Away Into You

7 Mascara

8 Been Insane

9 Skin Blues

10 Your Pussy's Glued To A Building On Fire

11 Blood On My Neck From Success

12 Ten To Butter Blood Voodoo

13 – 25 Usually Just A T-Shirt: Untitled

SMILE FROM THE STREET YOU HOLD

Birdman Records 1997

1 Enter A Uh
2 Other
3 Life's A Bath
4 A Fall Thru The Ground
5. Poppy Man
6 I May Again Know John
7 I'm Always
8 Nigger Song
9 Femininity
10 Breathe
11 More
12 For Air
13 Height Down
14 Well, I've Been
15 Smile From The Streets You Hold
16 I Can't See Until I See Your Eyes
17 Estress

TO RECORD ONLY WATER FOR TEN DAYS

Warner Brothers Feb 2001

1 Going Inside
2 Someone's
3 First Season
4 Wind Up Space
5 Away & Anywhere
6 Remain
7 Fallout
8 Ramparts
9 With No One
10 Murderers
11 Invisible Movement
12 Representing
13 In Rime
14 Saturation
15 Moments Have You

THE RED HOT CHILI PEPPERS Discography

ALBUMS

THE RED HOT CHILI PEPPERS 1984

1 True Men Don't Kill Coyotes
2 Baby Appeal
3 Buckle Down
4 Get Up And Jump
5 Why Don't You Love Me
6 Green Heaven
7 Mommy Where's Daddy
8 Out In LA
9 Police Helicopter
10 You Always Sing
11 Grand Pappy Du Plenty

UK RE-RELEASE EXTRA TRACKS

12 Get Up And Jump (Demo) 2:36
13 Police Helicopter (Demo)
14 Out In LA (Demo)
15 Green Heaven (Demo)
16 What It Is (aka Nina's Song)

FREAKY STYLEY 1985

1 Jungle Man
2 Hollywood
3 American Ghost Dance
4 If You Want Me To Stay
5 Nevermind
6 Freaky Styley
7 Blackeyed Blonde
8 The Brothers Cup
9 Battle Ship
10 Lovin' And Touchin'
11 Catholic School Girls Rule
12 Sex Rap
13 Thirty Dirty Birds
14 Yertle The Turtle

UK RE-RELEASE EXTRA TRACKS

15 Nevermind (Demo)
first released on *Out In LA*

16 Sex Rap (Demo)
first released on *Out In LA*
17 Freaky Styley (Original
instrumental long version)
Previously unreleased
18 Millionaires Against Hunger
B-side from "Taste The Pain"

THE UPLIFT MOFO PARTY PLAN 1987

1 Fight Like A Brave
2 Funky Crime
3 Me & My Friends
4 Backwoods
5 Skinny Sweaty Man
6 Behind The Sun
7 Subterranean Homesick Blues
8 Special Secret Song Inside
9 No Chump Love Sucker
10 Walkin' On Down The Road
11 Love Trilogy
12 Organic Anti-Beat Box Band

UK RE-RELEASE EXTRA TRACKS

13 Behind The Sun (Instrumental demo)
Previously unreleased
14 Me & My Friends (Instrumental demo)
Previously unreleased

The Abbey Road EP 1988

1 Fire
2 Backwoods – From *The Uplift Mofo Party Plan*
3 Catholic School Girls Rule – From *Freaky Styley*
4 Hollywood (Africa) – From *Freaky Styley*
5 True Men Don't Kill Coyotes – From *The Red Hot Chili Peppers*
Producers: Michael Beinhorn, George Clinton, Andy Gill

MOTHER'S MILK 1989

1 Good Time Boys
2 Higher Ground
3 Subway To Venus
4 Magic Johnson
5 Nobody Weird Like Me
6 Knock Me Down
7 Taste The Pain
8 Stone Cold Bush
9 Fire
10 Pretty Little Ditty
11 Punk Rock Classic
12 Sexy Mexican Maid
13 Johnny Kick A Hole In The Sky

UK RE-RELEASE EXTRA TRACKS

14 Song That Made Us What We Are Today (Demo)
15 Knock Me Down (Original long version) Previously unreleased
16 Sexy Mexican Maid
17 Salute To Kareem (Demo w/guitar track) Previously unreleased
18 Castles Made Of Sand (Live 11/21/89)
B-side of "Taste The Pain", previously reissued on *Out In LA*
19 Crosstown Traffic (Live 11/21/89)
Previously unreleased

BLOOD SUGAR SEX MAGIK 1991

1 Power of Equality
2 If You Have to Ask
3 Breaking the Girl
4 Funky Monks
5 Suck My Kiss
6 I Could Have Lied
7 Mellowship Slinky in B Major
8 The Righteous & The Wicked
9 Give It Away
10 Blood Sugar Sex Magik
11 Under The Bridge
12 Naked In The Rain

13 Apache Rose Peacock
14 Greeting Song
15 My Lovely Man
16 Sir Psycho Sexy
17 They're Red Hot

ONE HOT MINUTE 1995

1 Warped
2 Aeroplane
3 Deep Kick
4 My Friends
5 Coffee Shop
6 Pea
7 One Big Mob
8 Walkabout
9 Tearjerker
10 One Hot Minute
11 Falling Into Grace
12 Shallow Be Thy Game
13 Transcending

CALIFORNICATION 1999

1 Around The World
2 Parallel Universe
3 Scar Tissue
4 Otherside
5 Get On Top
6 Californication
7 Easily
8 Porcelain
9 Emit Remmus
10 I Like Dirt
11 This Velvet Glove
12 Savior
13 Purple Stain
14 Right On Time
15 Road Trippin'

BY THE WAY 2002

1 By The Way
2 Universally Speaking
3 This Is The Place
4 Dosed
5 Don't Forget Me
6 The Zephyr Song
7 Can't Stop
8 I Could Die For You
9 Midnight
10 Throw Away Your Television
11 Cabron

12 Tear
13 On Mercury
14 Minor Thing
15 Warm Tape
16 Venice Queen

SINGLES

1987

Fight Like A Brave
Fight Like A Brave
Fire

1989

Knock Me Down EP 1
Knock Me Down
Millionaires Against Hunger
Fire
Punk Rock Classic

Knock Me Down EP 2
Knock Me Down
Punk Rock Classic
Pretty Little Ditty

Unbridled Funk and Roll 4 Your Soul!
Taste The Pain
Millionaires Against Hunger
Castles
Higher Ground (Daddy-O Mix)

1990

Higher Ground 1
Politician (Mini Rap)
Higher Ground (Munchkin Mix)
Higher Ground (Dub Mix)
Mommy Where's Daddy

Higher Ground 2
Knock Me Down
Punk Rock Classic
Magic Johnson
Special Secret Song Inside

Taste The Pain
Taste The Pain (Album version)
Show Me Your Soul
Castles

If You Want Me To Stay EP
If You Want Me To Stay
Me & My Friends
Special Secret Song Inside

1992

Breaking The Bridge EP
Under The Bridge
Sikamikanico
Suck My Kiss
Search And Destroy

Breaking The Girl EP
Breaking The Girl
Fela's Cock (Previously unreleased)
Suck My Kiss (Live)
I Could Have Lied (Live)

1994

Give It Away
Give It Away (Single mix)
Give It Away (12-inch mix)
Search and Destroy
Give It Away (Rasta Mix)
Give It Away (Album version)

Under The Bridge EP (Re-release)
Under The Bridge
Sikamikanico
Suck My Kiss
Search And Destroy

1994

Soul To Squeeze
Soul To Squeeze
Nobody Weird Like Me
If You Have To Ask (Scott & Garth Mix)
Soul To Squeeze

Red Live Hot Rare Chili Remix Peppers Box
Live
1. Give It Away (Live)
2. Nobody Weird Like Me (Live)
3. Suck My Kiss (Live)
4. I Could Have Lied (Live)

Rare
1. Soul To Squeeze (Non-album track)
2. Fela's Cock (Non-album track)
3. Sikamikanico (Non-album track)
4. Search And Destroy (Non-album track)

Remix
1. Give It Away (12-inch mix)
2. Give It Away (Rasta Mix)
3. If You Have To Ask (The Disco Krisco Mix)
4. If You Have To Ask (Scott & Garth Mix)
5. If You Have To Ask (The Friday Night Fever Blister Mix)

1995
Warped
Warped (Edit)
Pea (Album version)
Melancholy Mechanics
My Friends
My Friends
Coffee Shop
Let's Make Evil
Stretch

1996
Aeroplane
Aeroplane
Backwoods
Transcending
Me & My Friends
Love Rollercoaster
Love Rollercoaster
Lesbian Seagull (Engelbert Humperdinck)

1999
Scar Tissue
Scar Tissue
Gong Li
Instrumental #1

1999
Californication
Californication
End of Show Brisbane
I Could Have Lied
End Of Show State College
Around The World
Me & My Friends (Non-album track)
Yertle Trilogy (Non-album track)

2000
Otherside
Otherside
How Strong
Road Trippin'

Road Trippin'
Road Trippin'
Californication (Live)
Blood Sugar Sex Magik (Live)
Under The Bridge (Live)
If You Had To Ask (Live)

2002
By the Way UK 2 x CD
By The Way
Time
Teenager In Love
By The Way
Search And Destroy (live)
What Is Soul (live)
Zephyr Song
Zephyr Song
Out Of Range
Universally Speaking UK 2 x CD
Universally Speaking
By The Way (Live acoustic)
Don't Forget Me (Live)
Universally Speaking
Slowly Deeply
Universally Speaking (Enhanced video)

2003
Fortune Faded
Fortune Faded (Album version)
Eskimo (Non-album track)
Bunker Hill (Non-album track)
Can't Stop UK 2 x CD
Can't Stop (New mix)
If You Have To Ask (Live)
Christ Church Fireworks Music
Can't Stop
Right On Time (Live)
Nothing To Lose (Live)

VIDEO
1990
Psychedelic Sexfunk Live from Heaven
Live concert footage and backstage shenanigans from the *Mother's Milk* tour filmed at Long Beach Arena, California. Tracks performed include: "Stone Cold Bush", "Good Time Boys", "Nevermind" and "Knock Me Down"

1990
Positive Mental Octopus
One live track – "Fire" – the rest are "conceptual" pieces
Taste The Pain
Higher Ground
Knock Me Down
Fight Like A Brave
Fire
Catholic School Girls Rule
Jungle Man
True Men Don't Kill Coyotes

1992
What Hits!?
Tracks include "Behind The Sun", "Show Me Your Soul", "Stone Cold Bush", "Special Secret Song" and "Knock Me Down"

1997
Funky Monks
Live recording performances from the *Blood Sugar Sex Magik* album

2001
Off the Map
Recorded live on the last night of the *Californication* world tour. Tracks include "Suck My Kiss", "Californication", "Blood Sugar Sex Magik", "Scar Tissue", "Right On Time", "Under The Bridge" and "Me & My Friends".

2002
By The Way (DVD Single)

2003
Greatest Hits and Videos
Under The Bridge
Give It Away
Californication
Scar Tissue
Soul To Squeeze
Otherside
Suck My Kiss
By The Way
Parallel Universe
Breaking The Girl
My Friends
Higher Ground
Universally Speaking

Road Trippin'
Fortune Faded
Save The Population
Higher Ground
Suck My Kiss
Give It Away
Under The Bridge
Soul To Squeeze
Aeroplane
My Friends
Around The World
Scar Tissue
Otherside
Californication
Road Trippin'
By The Way
The Zephyr Song
Can't Stop
Universally Speaking

2003
Live At Slane DVD
By The Way
Scar Tissue
Around The World
Universally Speaking
Parallel Universe
Zephyr Song
Throw Away Your Television
Havana Affair
Otherside
Purple Stain
Don't Forget Me
Right On Time
Can't Stop
Venice Queen
Give It Away
Californication
Under The Bridge
Power Of Equality

Compilations
1992
WHAT HITS!?
Higher Ground
Fight Like A Brave
Behind The Sun
Me And My Friends
Backwoods
True Men Don't Kill Coyotes
Fire

Get Up And Jump
Knock Me Down
Under The Bridge
Show Me Your Soul
If You Want Me To Stay
Hollywood
Jungle Man
The Brothers Cup
Taste The Pain
Catholic School Girls Rule
Johnny Kick A Hole In The Sky

1994
OUT IN LA
Higher Ground (12-inch vocal mix)
Hollywood (Africa) (Extended
  Dance Mix)
If You Want Me to Stay
  (Pink Mustang Mix)
Behind the Sun (Ben Grosse Remix)
Castles Made of Sand (Live)
Special Secret Song Inside
F.U. (Live)
Get Up And Jump (Demo version)
Out In LA (Demo version)
Green Heaven (Demo version)
Police Helicopter (Demo version)
Nevermind (Demo version)
Sex Rap (Demo version)
Blues For Meister
You Always Sing The Same
Stranded
Flea Fly
What It Is
Deck the Halls

1994
GREATEST HITS (EMI)
Behind The Sun
Johnny Kick A Hole In The Sky
Me & My Friends
Fire
True Men Don't Kill Coyotes
Higher Ground
Knock Me
Fight Like A Brave
Taste The Pain
If You Want Me To Stay

2003
GREATEST HITS
(WARNER BROS)
1 Under The Bridge
2 Give It Away
3 Californication
4 Scar Tissue
5 Soul To Squeeze
6. Otherside
(Flea~Kiedis/Frusciante/Kiedis/Smith)
7 Suck My Kiss
8 By The Way
9 Parallel Universe
10 Breaking The Girl
11 My Friends
12 Higher Ground
13 Universally Speaking
14 Road Trippin'
15 Fortune Faded
16 Save The Population

The Red Hot Chili Peppers appear on:
ORIGINAL SOUNDTRACK
SAY ANYTHING (1989)
Taste The Pain
ORIGINAL SOUNDTRACK
PRETTY WOMAN (1990)
Show Me Your Soul

ORIGINAL SOUNDTRACK
WAYNE'S WORLD (1992)
Sikamikanico

ORIGINAL SOUNDTRACK
MIGHTY MORPHIN POWER
RANGERS... (1995)
Higher Ground

ORIGINAL SOUNDTRACK
TWISTER (1996)
Melancholy Mechanics

ORIGINAL SOUNDTRACK
BEAVIS AND BUTT-HEAD DO
AMERICA (1997)
Love Rollercoaster

CENTER STAGE (2000)
Higher Ground

⬚Chronology⬚

1962

Anthony Kiedis born on November 1, Grand Rapids, MI Flea (Michael Balzary) born on October 16, Melbourne, Australia Hillel Slovak born on April 13, Haifa, Israel Jack Irons born July 18, Los Angeles, CA Chad Smith born October 25, St Paul, MN.

1967

Hillel Slovak's family move to Los Angeles

1970

John Frusciante is born on March 5, New York, NY

1973

Anthony Kiedis moves to LA to live with his father.

1977

Flea and Anthony meet at Fairfax High School. Hillel and Jack begin playing in their first band, Chain Reaction.

1978

Chain Reaction becomes Anthym; bass player Todd Strasman leaves and is replaced by Flea.

1980

Anthony, Flea, Hillel and Jack all graduate from Fairfax High.

1981

Flea quits Anthym and joins the LA punk band Fear. Anthym change their name to What Is This?!

1983

Anthony Kiedis, Flea, Hillel Slovak and Jack Irons perform a one-off show at LA's Rhythm Lounge as Tony Flow and the Miraculously Majestic Masters of Mayhem. The following week they return as The Red Hot Chili Peppers. Within one month of recording their first demo tape, the band secures a seven-album deal with EMI/America

1984

Because Jack Irons and Hillel Slovak have prior loyalty to What Is This?!, who are also about to be signed to a major label, they leave The Red Hot Chili Peppers. They are replaced by guitarist Jack Sherman and drummer Cliff Martinez. The band record their debut album with producer Andy Gill. The first, self-titled album is released on EMI

1985

Hillel Slovak quits What Is This?! and joins the Chili Peppers. The band record their second album with George Clinton producing. Album *Freaky Styley* is released and the band play in the UK for the first time.

1986

Cliff Martinez quits and is replaced by Jack Irons, who has quit What Is This?! Sixteen-year-old John Frusciante sees his first Red Hot Chili Peppers gig at the Variety Arts Center in LA.

1987

Third album *The Uplift Mofo Party Plan*, produced by Michael Beinhorn, is released and the band embark on an extensive tour schedule.

1988

"The Abbey Road EP" is released. The band successfully tour the UK. Hillel dies of a heroin overdose in June. Jack Irons decides to leave the band. Former Dead Kennedys drummer DH Peligro replaces him. Guitarist Duane "Blackbyrd" McKnight replaces Hillel on guitar. Both are soon replaced; McKnight by John Frusciante and Peligro by Chad Smith. The band record *Mother's Milk* with Beinhorn producing again.

1989

Mother's Milk is their best selling album to date and delivers the band hits with "Higher Ground" and "Knock Me Down".

1990

Flea and Smith are arrested at a concert in Florida and charged with sexually harassing a woman during a show. The band sign a new record deal with Warner Brothers.

1991

Rick Rubin is engaged as producer on the fifth album ⬚ The band record at a house in Laurel Canyon, LA ⬚ *Blood Sugar Sex Magik* is released and sells a million copies before the end of the year.

1992

During a world tour, in Tokyo, John Frusciante announces he is leaving the band. He is eventually replaced by Arik Marshall. *Blood Sugar Sex Magik* reaches #3 in the US. "Under The Bridge" hits #2 in the US. Lollapolooza tour opens at Shoreline Amphitheatre. Arik Marshall is replaced by Jesse Tobias. By the end of the year, *Blood Sugar Sex Magik* has sold nearly 3 million copies.

1993

The Red Hot Chili Peppers appear on *The Simpsons*. Jesse Tobias is replaced by former Jane's Addiction guitar player Dave Navarro. River Phoenix dies in front of the Viper Room. Flea diagnosed with Chronic Fatigue Syndrome and ordered to rest for 12 months.

1994

The band play at Woodstock. The band start recording a new album

1995

The new album *One Hot Minute* is finally released. Chad breaks his wrist playing baseball; part of the world tour is cancelled.

1996

The band's cover version of the Ohio Players' 1975 hit "Love

Rollercoaster" appears in the movie *Beavis and Butt-Head Do America*

1997

Both Anthony and Chad have motorbike accidents within weeks of one another. Rumours circulate that the band are on the verge of splitting. Jane's Addiction go on a reunion tour, with Dave Navarro playing guitar and Flea on bass. Dave Navarro announces that he doesn't want to play the forthcoming Chili Peppers winter tour.

1998

Dave Navarro "leaves" the band. John Frusciante, having spent the six years since quitting the band in a narcotic haze, rejoins them. The new old line-up makes its official debut at the Tibetan Freedom Concert

1999

Californication is released in June. The band tour the world promoting the album. By the end of the year, the album is multi-platinum across the world.

2000

The band tour the world for most of the year.   The Chilis win a Grammy for Best rock song for "Scar Tissue".

2001

Huge gigs around the planet continue, including the Rock In Rio festival with an audience of 200,000. Work starts on writing and recording of the next album.

2002

By The Way is released worldwide in July.

2003

The first four Chili Pepper albums are re-released and re-mastered, with bonus tracks. *Greatest Hits And Videos* album released, including two new songs. "Fortune Faded" released. Flea announces that the band have written 15 new songs

2004

John Frusciante's fourth solo album due out

Index